Endorsements

"For years I have encouraged Michelle to write this book because she is the most gracious leader I know. I treasure her noble character and heart for Jesus. Everything she does as a leader is almost always about serving others. She lives out the truths captured here and has taught many how to thrive in the calling of God on their lives. Her book will do you tremendous good."

GREGORY HASWELL
Northlands Church

"Michelle's leadership is unlike any I've ever known. Her wise words bring us all higher. She leads with peace in every season, and her friendship has led me into deeper realms of trust in Him. Living Refreshed isn't just a title, it's who she is. This book is a gift."

RACHEL BROWN
Be Still Ministries

"Living Refreshed is good mentoring at its best. It's written with layers of grace, making it relatable, practical, and best of all, doable. I've benefited countless times from Michelle's wise counsel, and the words in this book mirror her life. She shares her mistakes vulnerably and invites us to share in her victories, calling us all to lead with complete freedom."

KAREN RASMUSSEN
Better Together Ministry

"May the Lord encourage you to believe that He is ready to do for you what He is doing for Michelle, to empower you to live the refreshed life. In these pages, you will find the secrets to avoiding burn out and nurturing resilience."

DR SUSAN HILLIS
World without Orphans, Executive Team

"Michelle Haswell is the real deal. Her vibrant relationship with God is evident on every page of this book. She is that rare leader whose life both behind the scenes and in the spotlight is marked by the same excellence. Whether you have been in leadership for years or are just now beginning to sense God's call, this book will be a gift to you."

BETH TEMPLETON
Hope at Home

"I've had the pleasure of knowing Michelle for over 25 years and can confidently say that she lives and leads the very essence of her book. Living Refreshed is a practical training tool for women in leadership and serves as a guide for young leaders and a great refresher for veterans."

PASTOR LESLEY A CAMPBELL
Harvey Campbell Ministries

"Michelle's ministry always brings me encouragement, healing, and guidance. She never fails to evoke courage in my life. It is a privilege to have her life-lessons with Jesus collected in this book. Living Refreshed is a must-read for every woman in leadership."

LUCINDA RASMUSSEN,
Naestved City Church, Denmark

"In 1993 I accepted an invitation from the Lord to listen, observe, learn from, and to apply the loving wisdom He has imparted to my mentor and friend, Michelle. This has been a consistent, silk cushion for me to personally fall back on through 26 years of being challenged, inspired, and encouraged! Michelle, you delight my soul... women everywhere will "Live Refreshed" as they hear our Lord speak through your words."

BRIDGET ELLWOOD
The Bridge Church for all Nations, Pickering, Canada

"Living Refreshed is a powerful read on how to stay healthy and empowered in ministry. It is packed with wisdom and Biblical truth that will sustain any leader who takes them to heart."

JEN GRENFELL
Free Life Church, Virginia

Michelle Haswell is a gifted leader who is paving the way for women leading in their sphere of influence. Her book, *Living Refreshed*, is packed with wisdom and authenticity and, I believe that as you read her words you will lean into and embrace who you are and what you were born for. This book is a testament to Michelle's consistency and commitment to pursue her best life.

TES JAHNIG
Senior Pastor Linc Church, South Africa

Thanks to:

Ray & Cindy: For the gift of time overlooking the ocean.

Frank & Patty: For providing a beautiful setting to write.

Jenny: For valuable insight and help with key statements.

Lindsay: For sharing your strength and helping format key statements.

Beth: For your help with the editing.

And to the many who have prayed for me while writing, I'm deeply thankful for each of you.

Living Refreshed

Empowering women with

tools for leadership

MICHELLE HASWELL

Deep Roots Press 2019

Cover design by Jesse Palmer

Dedications

This book is dedicated to four people who have my heart and have taught me about the Lord's great love for us in many different ways.

To my husband, Greg, my best friend, ministry and covenant partner. Life with you continues to be an exciting adventure in the Lord. I respect and honor you as an incredible leader and the best Bible teacher I know. I wouldn't have been able to complete this book without your practical help and your unwavering faith in me. I love you with all my heart and thank the Lord for you daily.

To my beautiful daughter, Nicole, you're one in a million and I count you as not only my daughter of whom I could not be prouder, but also a friend and ministry partner. You are one with much wisdom and discernment and also a delightful sense of humor. Thank you for your heart for people and His bride. Thank you for your time and expertise in editing this book. You're the best at it and I'm thankful for your investment and advice.

To Tyler, my son in love, I have loved you from the moment I met you. I am so thankful to the Lord for bringing you into our family and loving our daughter and granddaughter so well. Thank you for your Kingdom heart and for always giving your best to Him.

To my precious Evangeline, you are a beautiful reminder of the Lord's kindness. Thank you for initiating us into the world of grandparenting and for being a joy bringer wherever you are. Your laughter and love of life is contagious, and the joy of the Lord already shines through you. I trust that the pages of this book will be of value to you in the years to come.

Table of Contents

PART 1
Caring for yourself

PART 2

Strong Foundations

PART 3

Relationships

CHAPTER 13

CHAPTER 14

CHAPTER 15

PART 4

Dressed to Lead

CHAPTER 16

Foreword

Greg and Michelle Haswell are some of the good people! Good people who are doing life well. We have done ministry together, eaten good food together and counseled together. It is such a privilege to forward Michelle's book "Living Refreshed".

We have seen the toll that is taken on anyone touching the inner courts of ministry. While we are huge advocates of "all Jesus people are ministers", there is a different requirement, skill set and sensitivity to leading in "full time ministry". Michelle has written an excellent tool to encourage, exhort, and remind us all of how important it is to lead well. Having the position of leadership is not to be taken lightly, it is full of serpentine curves, cliff jumping, rapid riding and all at the same rewarding and a calling to be taken seriously.

This book is more about glory management rather than sin management. John 17:4, "Jesus said I have glorified you here on earth and finished everything that you have called me to do." Michelle is leading others to lead and love just like Jesus, to glorify the father. To burn brightly without burning out!

Michelle is writing out of a heart full of wisdom, and from a place of vulnerability, honesty and at times humor. She is providing helpful tools to run the race well. We really appreciate the practical applications at the end of each section that allow the reader to not only read, but think, ponder and then take action.

This book is geared towards women but is not just for women. It is for all believers, marketplace ministers, ministers in every walk of life!

Leif and Jennifer Hetland

Introduction

A t the young age of seventeen, I fell in love with Greg Haswell. At the outset of our relationship, he told me that he could not promise me an ordinary life but that he could promise me an exciting one. He has been true to his word. Greg knew God had called him to full time ministry in the church. And I knew he was the one I wanted to marry, so this call included me. Together, we have lead youth ministry, student college ministry, and a mission school. We started radio stations, a telephone crisis counselling service, national church leadership groups and many smaller groups. We have pastored on the staff of a large church, led our own church to a place of significance in the city, and pioneered a church in a country that was foreign to us but is now very much home. We continue to love the local church and minister in the nations as the Lord leads. Alongside the ministry, I was a school teacher and served as head of faculty in an elementary school for four years, which I loved!

As you move through the pages of this book, see it as an invitation from me to you to share some of what I have learned and have found helpful in over thirty years of ministry. My lens is the local church, but much of what pertains to leadership will apply across different spheres. I have purposefully divided the content into sections so that there will be something relevant for anyone picking this up.

Over the years, I have learned so much from many different mentors and have been eternally thankful for their wisdom and practical insight.

I do not, by any means, claim to have it all together, but my hope is that this book will be one of many tools in your hand as you navigate your journey. I want to emphasize that though we learn from one another, His voice is always the primary one we seek. Holy Spirit remains our best counselor.

May these practical tools strengthen and anchor you as you lead in your sphere of influence.

Part 1

CARING FOR YOURSELF

When I think of things I wish I knew as a young leader; this one comes to mind first: I cannot give to others what I do not have.

If you ask me for one hundred dollars, and I have nothing in my bank account, I cannot meet your need. In the same way, I am unable to give emotional or spiritual support if I'm a burned-out leader.

When we care for ourselves, staying refreshed in our relationship with God, setting healthy boundaries, and stewarding our time and energy, we will lead with excellence. This section dives into self-care, because you can't share what you don't have and because when you're full, you can feed others well.

1

Do I have what it takes?

Secret Place Ministry

My morning ritual looks something like this: Turn off alarm, check phone for news of family overseas, make tea, enjoy time with the Lord, and then address outstanding messages.

By Tuesday, there's usually a good number of texts from dear people in the congregation needing answers, comfort, or a place to voice a complaint. We encourage people to complain up, so it's good that they come directly to me with issues on their heart, but I find myself asking, "Do I have what they need? Will they find what they're needing, and is it mine to have the answers? How do I respond in helpful way?"

Most days there will be a fair number of texts or phone messages that need to be returned, along with an answer or a fresh perspective. Sometimes, these will be reports of something wonderful that God has done (my favorites!). There will be emails with great testimonies and some with well-meaning suggestions of how to better lead a certain area of ministry or how the worship is too loud or there wasn't a gluten-free option at a church event.

To each one, the need to be heard is important. The answer they receive from me might not be what they had hoped for, but I do try to give a respectful answer either personally or through our administration.

All of these demands require being filled up in the secret place so that I can give from overflow.

Psalm 91 tells us that if we stay in the secret place of the Most High we will remain stable and fixed under the shadow of the Almighty.

I don't believe it's possible to remain in leadership for an extended period of time without this key Biblical truth. Without accessing the Lord's rest and learning to live in His Presence, we will surely run dry and most likely burn out, as many sadly do.

Before I can feed others, I need to eat fresh bread from Heaven so that I can give from my overflow. I need to receive so that I can feed. Countless times, I have read a scripture in the morning, only to find that later in the day it's the very thing that someone else needed.

When I live full, it's easy to pour out.

When I live full, it's easy to pour out. When I neglect my own intimate relationship with the Lord, I'll eventually burn out. This is never our Father's intention. We find Jesus withdrawing often to hear His Father's voice and then responding only to what He had told Him. His is the most fruitful ministry the earth has ever seen, and we are offered the same and even greater!

Mark 1:35 NIV "Very early in the morning, while it was still dark, Jesus got up, left the house and went off to a solitary place to pray"

We are designed to be firmly planted in His love for us.

Heidi Baker says, "all fruitfulness flows from intimacy."

Psalm 1 tells us that trees that are planted by the streams of water produce fruit in season and their leaves do not wither. A tree does not strive to produce fruit but naturally does so if it is well-tended and planted in good soil. Our Father's intent is that we are firmly planted in His love for us, receiving fresh water and nourishment from Him that brings forth good fruit from our lives. When this is where we live, we'll be well-fed so that we can feed others well. We will hear His voice saying, "this is the way, walk in it." Our leadership will be in response to His voice and not in reaction to every need. We will see His grace abound because He always provides where He leads.

What happens in the secret place?

We Wait

Psalm 62:1 AMPC "FOR GOD alone my soul waits in silence; from Him comes my salvation."

Isaiah 40:31 AMPC "But those who wait for the Lord [who expect, look for, and hope in Him] shall change and renew their strength and power; they shall lift their wings and mount up [close to God] as eagles [mount up to the sun]; they shall run and not be weary, they shall walk and not faint or become tired"

One of the definitions of "waiting" is to stay or rest in expectation. For most of us this is not easy because we live in a fast-paced world, and as leaders, there is always the next thing to take care of or another person who needs our attention. Too often, our time set aside to spend focused on the Lord is shared with a response to a text message or a phone call or an email. Waiting on the Lord and turning off all other distractions is not an easy discipline, but I believe it's an essential one if we're going to remain strong.

The scripture's answer to weariness is waiting. Practice the discipline of just waiting in silence and being aware of His Presence.

We Worship

Psalm 40:3 AMPC "And He has put a new song in my mouth, a song of praise to our God. Many shall see and fear (revere and worship) and put their trust and confident reliance in the Lord"

Psalm 95:6 AMPC "O come, let us worship and bow down, let us kneel before the Lord our Maker [in reverent praise and supplication]."

I play worship music in my home or office almost all day. A few minutes of engaging in worship will change my perspective from negative to positive & from feeling defeated to full of faith. Many times, on my way to a meeting with someone or when trusting God for a breakthrough, I will listen to worship because it purposefully turns my attention towards Heaven.

Praise of our King will usher in peace and release stress. It will cause a mountain to become a molehill, and it will be a refuge in the storm. We were created to worship our King.

Praise and worship are weapons in our hands against the enemy. In 1 Chronicles 20:22, Jehoshaphat appointed singers and when they began to sing and praise, the Lord set ambushes against the enemy. When we make worship a priority, we will be the mighty warriors on behalf of our people that God has called and positioned us to be.

If you need a breakthrough, turn to worship.

We Read

> Hebrews 4:12 NIV "For the word of God is alive and active. Sharper than any double-edged sword, it penetrates even to dividing soul and spirit, joints and marrow; it judges the thoughts and attitudes of the heart."

The Word of God is a treasure and a great source of strength to me. His promises in the Word have been anchors in my life which I stand on when nothing makes sense in my circumstances. I pray the Word over those I lead and over my own life.

Fresh revelation from the word of God needs to be in us so that it can be released through us.

If we're going to be leaders who release hope and life, it's imperative that we have fresh bread from the Word of God to share. It needs to be in us so that it can be released through us. Declaring the Word over circumstances and people is what affects change to bring things into Biblical alignment. The Word declared will bring peace and move mountains.

Jesus used the Word as a weapon when tempted by the enemy in the desert.

Matthew 4:1-4 NIV "Then Jesus was led by the Spirit into the wilderness to be tempted by the devil. After fasting forty days and forty nights, he was hungry. The tempter came to him and said, "If you are the Son of God, tell these stones to become bread." Jesus answered, "It is written: 'Man shall not live on bread alone, but on every word that comes from the mouth of God.'

We declare

Here's what declaring looks like in my life: at times, I've taken photographs of my family and put them on the floor and walked around declaring the promises of God over them and what is theirs by right as children of God. I can declare healing or financial provision because Jesus took their sickness and He is their provider. I can declare breakthrough because God is the God of the breakthrough. There are times when we walk around our church sanctuary and declare out loud the words & promises God has spoken over us. If you are a parent, ask the Lord how He sees your children and pray that over them. If they go through a challenging season, declare the truth of who God says they are. We can declare the favor of God over our businesses, our families, our bodies, and our churches. I believe firmly in the power of declaration because I see it all over the scriptures beginning in Genesis.

Genesis 1:3 NIV "And God said, "Let there be light," and there was light."

Genesis 1:9 NIV "And God said, "Let the water under the sky be gathered to one place, and let dry ground appear." And it was so."

His words in our mouth spoken out loud have the power to bring life into what appears dead. The prophet Ezekiel had to open his mouth and declare the word of the Lord over the dry bones.

Ezekiel 37:4-5 NIV "Then he said to me, "Prophesy to these bones and say to them, 'Dry bones, hear the word of the LORD! This is what the Sovereign LORD says to these bones: I will make breath enter you, and you will come to life."

Be a leader who is filled with His word and declares it out loud, and you will be a leader who brings forth fruit and releases breakthrough in many lives.

Reflection

1. How do you fill yourself up so that you can meet the needs of those you lead? *Go fr daily walks.*

2. What, in these pages, would you consider adding to your personal routine? *Turning off Distractions*

3. Take a few minutes and practice some of the four steps mentioned in this chapter.

We wait

We Wrship

We read

We Declare

Asking the Lrd how he sees our children and pray that aur them.

Remember . . .

When you live full, it's easy to pour out.

Fresh revelation from the word of God needs to be in you so that it

can be released through you.

2

No need to burn out

Filling my emotional cup

Driving through Atlanta in rush hour traffic, I'm deciding whether to drive through Starbucks to get a strong cup of coffee for this commute. I'm on my way home from a two-hour counseling appointment, and I'm ready to take a long nap. But in the back of my head, I often hear my own accusing voice, "What's wrong with me? I should be energized right now! Maybe I'm not getting enough sleep?" Even after one appointment, I still underestimate the emotional and spiritual draw that others' needs, and heartaches can have on me. I can easily forget that I'm taking on spiritual giants as I come against hopelessness and sickness and lack.

Many times, we have done some heavy lifting in a realm we cannot see.

As leaders, we don't realize that many times we have done some heavy lifting in a realm we cannot see. Wonder why people leave your office with a smile? Because you have helped lift what was weighing them down! You've partnered with the Lord as He said we are to do.

The gospels tell us that we will lay hands on the sick and they will recover. They tell us that we will drive out demons in His Name. They also show us Jesus retreating to be alone with His Father.

This scripture has always fascinated me:

"And a woman was there who had been subject to bleeding for twelve years, but no one could heal her. She came up behind him and touched the edge of his cloak, and immediately her bleeding stopped. "Who touched me?" Jesus asked. When they all denied it, Peter said, "Master, the people are crowding and pressing against you." But Jesus said, "Someone touched me; I know that power has gone out from me." Luke 8:43-46 NIV

Jesus knew power had gone from Him, which means power needed to be replaced.

Do you ever wonder why you can feel exhausted after an intense time of ministry or leadership? Because power has gone from you.

We need to learn to recharge our emotional batteries. Jesus, our perfect leader, demonstrated the value of this. Amidst healing the sick, driving out demons, feeding thousands and teaching His disciples, He withdrew often from the crowds and the demands of ministry to find solitude and time with His Father. It's a myth that only negative tasks drain us. In fact, it's often the God-ordained things that burn us out the fastest, simply because we've failed to set boundaries on our energy output. Jesus was setting people free and still needed to withdraw. He invites us to follow His example.

Matthew 14:22-23 NIV "Immediately Jesus made the disciples get into the boat and go on ahead of him to the other side, while he dismissed the crowd. After he had dismissed them, he went up on a mountainside by himself to pray."

Jesus never disregarded the practical needs of rest and refreshment.

John 6:5 NIV "When Jesus looked up and saw a great crowd coming toward him, he said to Philip, "Where shall we buy bread for these people to eat?"

Emotional resources require replenishment.

Replenishing our emotional resources is one the most spiritual things we can do. Before Jesus performed the miracles, he took care of the practical need of rest and refreshment as He fed the crowds. We see this pattern throughout the Scriptures.

1 Kings 17:2 -5 NIV "Then the word of the LORD came to Elijah: "Leave here, turn eastward and hide in the Kerith Ravine, east of the Jordan. You will drink from the brook, and I have directed the ravens to supply you with food there." So he did what the Lord had told him. He went to the Kerith Ravine, east of the Jordan, and stayed there. The ravens brought him bread and meat in the morning and bread and meat in the evening, and he drank from the brook."

In this passage, the Lord gives Elijah a time of rest as He feeds him with fresh bread, meat, and water from the brook. The Lord led Elijah to a much-needed time of replenishment by providing a place of hiding and fresh food.

> John 12:1 NIV "Six days before the Passover, Jesus came to Bethany, where Lazarus lived, whom Jesus had raised from the dead. 2 Here a dinner was given in Jesus' honor. Martha served, while Lazarus was among those reclining at the table with him. 3 Then Mary took about a pint of pure nard, an expensive perfume; she poured it on Jesus' feet and wiped his feet with her hair. And the house was filled with the fragrance of the perfume"

Here, we find Jesus going to have a meal with close friends in Bethany. Mary, Martha, and Lazarus were some of the people in His life who filled His emotional cup and provided a place where Jesus could rest. We all need to have some Bethany places in our lives.

Sadly, there are too many leaders in ministry and all other spheres who have burned out for Jesus, which is certainly not what He ever intended.

With this in mind, it's most helpful to identify what replenishes your emotional resources. Maybe it's a walk outside in nature or getting alone with a good book. Maybe it's tea or coffee with a friend. It will be different for each one of us., but it's important to figure it out and make space for it in our schedules. When we prioritize rest and replenishment, we honor Jesus's perfect example.

Reflection

1. Identify those things that help strengthen you emotionally. Practice at least two this week. *Have lunch with a friend. Sit in silence.*

2. Make a list of the people in your life that refresh you and make time to fit them into your schedule.

This group, Christian women
My friend Jenny
Susan Phelphs, Posturing Together
Dena

Remember . . .

Jesus never disregarded the practical needs of rest and refreshment.

Emotional resources require replenishment.

3

I'm tired but there's still a lot to do

Recognizing what drains my emotional cup

It is possible to be spiritually strong and emotionally spent. Unhealthy, but possible.

Most leaders will find themselves here at least once because they are so passionate to do what the Lord has called them to. It takes wisdom to guard against getting to this place.

A warning sign for me is when I'm not regulating my emotions well. I feel frustrated with people and give short, curt responses that hurt. I have personally been on the receiving end of harsh words from leaders who are burned out. I have also been the one to deliver words with impatience and frustration because my cup was close to empty.

But here's the stark reality: we don't have license to hurt people just because we haven't been good stewards of our emotional health. We have to learn to take responsibility to replenish our emotional cup so that we can minister God's peace in whatever role He's called us to.

For the sake of others, we need to guard our emotional well-being and identify what causes us exhaustion. I have learned that multiple intense meetings over a number of days can drain my emotional cup to a point where I cannot give each person what they are needing from me.

Because I understand my responsibility is to pour into those I lead, I will not schedule more than two intense meetings in a day. It is unwise and will eventually be detrimental to both my emotional and physical well-being if I keep pouring into others and do not allow time to be replenished myself.

If I continually set a hot water kettle to boil but never replace the water level, it will burn out. There will always be one more need, one more person who needs help. When I am meeting those with deep needs, I make sure that I have some time between each appointment to give the situation to the Lord, so as not to carry more than He is requiring of me.

Learn how to say a gracious no.

We all have different capacities in different areas. There is no formula here, except what works well for you to do what you are called to in a way that does not cause you to burn out or lose your joy.

It's imperative that we learn how to say a gracious no. "Thank you so much for inviting me, but right now I do not have bandwidth to be involved here," works well for me. There will always be another project or activity to commit to, many being things that we would enjoy. A mature leader will first determine whether this is something they need to give their time to. We might ask ourselves the question, "Does this opportunity line up with the season I'm in?" This can be identified by taking note of our current responsibilities and what direction the Lord is giving us.

If you're dealing with an elderly parent or a child who is needing extra attention, it would seem unwise to offer much of your personal time to someone else's project or ongoing need. This is a season where you are needed to serve your family well. Maybe you're about to pioneer a new business and someone asks you to help them restructure theirs. Your time in this season would be best served in getting your own business established and then you can put more time into someone else's.

When our daughter was much younger and we were invited to minister away from home, I would only accompany Greg on a few of the trips or we would take her with us if that was an option. I declined a lot of travel opportunities because I believed it was best for me to be at home with her in that season of our lives.

Now, years later, Greg and I are in a different season and travel together most of the time. Seasons change and the things we say no to now might well be a yes later on. I have asked these questions when making these decisions: "Will my top priorities suffer if I make this commitment?" and "Do I have the emotional resources to give?"

Giving beyond my margin will lead to exhaustion!

Giving out of season and beyond the margin we have will lead to exhaustion, and this is often rooted in the inability to say no. Knowing what we have to give is vital to our emotional health. In Acts 3, Peter and John knew that they did not have finances to give. They also knew that they did have healing to give to the crippled man.

Acts 3:6 NIV "Silver and gold I do not have but what I do have I give to you. In the name of Jesus Christ of Nazareth, walk"

It is helpful to identify what we have to give and what we don't in any season of our lives.

Reflection

1. What areas in your life require you to say a no right now?
   Volunteering

2. In what areas do you feel you are giving from an empty cup?
   Take time to prayerfully ask the Lord what you are to commit
   to at this time. *I feel the Lord put this troubled child in my life to care for.*

3. What are two things you do have to give in your current season?

Remember . . .

It is possible to be spiritually strong and emotionally spent.

The more depleted you are, the more careful you have to be with how you respond to others.

You don't have license to hurt people merely because you have not taken care of yourself emotionally.

Giving beyond your margin will lead to exhaustion.

4

Move, Eat, Sleep

Caring for yourself practically

3 John 2:1 AMPC "Beloved I pray that you may prosper in every way and that your body may keep well, even as I know your soul keeps well and prospers"

Our destinies in God have been set and He has good works planned for each of us to walk in. I believe we are meant to find great satisfaction as we walk in His ways.

A. Stay Active

Just as we pursue spiritual and emotional wellness, it benefits us and those we lead when we pursue physical health. So many leaders experience physical distress because they've not been careful to keep themselves emotionally and physically healthy. They push past concerning symptoms in the name of productivity, but in the end, neglect of their body's practical needs ends up costing them much more time in the long run.

Set healthy boundaries in this area of physical health. It will only enhance your ability to walk the path set before you.

As a child at school, I was usually the last one picked for any sports team because athletics were not high on my skill set. During cross country season, I often hoped for a legitimate reason to miss that particular day—with little luck. As an adult, I became more aware of the health benefits of regular exercise and realized the value of finding different physical activities that would help me stay fit and that were also enjoyable.

I do have great admiration for those who are naturally athletic and strong in this area. It's something I have to work at. Taking a long walk, whether with a friend or alone, listening to worship music, is one of the ways I fill my emotional cup. It's a mental break from everyday demands.

Identify what works for you personally and make it a regular part of your routine.

This might be an area in your life where you're doing really well, and some of you might be in a season where this is not possible due to varying circumstances. This is no-guilt, no-judgment advice.

I do believe that exercise contributes to your overall health and longevity in your leadership role. When your season allows, I would encourage you to pursue a form of exercise that will benefit you and that you can enjoy. (If you have not exercised for a while, consult your doctor before starting a new exercise routine).

B. Fuel Your Body

There are so many options and diets and suggested restrictions as to what we should and should not eat. I'm not going to deal with any of this as that is yours to decide what works best for you personally. I will say that taking care of ourselves should include a lifestyle of fueling our bodies well.

As a leader in any capacity, you probably have many opportunities and invitations to eat out at various functions. Greg and I spend much of our time meeting with people over meals and visiting in homes. As we minister in different nations, we love to experience the local cuisine. So much meaningful connection takes place around a dinner table. As a child, I spent five years in Europe where meals can go on for hours around a table of warm conversation and good food.

There is something intimate and special about having people around your table. Jesus modeled the value of this, and we see Him sharing many meals throughout the gospels. He eats with Levi the tax collector, he goes to the house of Zacchaeus for a meal, he feeds the five thousand, and of course has the all-important last supper with His disciples, to name a few. Ministry and leadership will involve many meals as we connect with those we lead.

Meaningful connection happens

when we eat together.

Because meals are integral to connection, I aim to be careful with what I eat, because I want to be as healthy as possible. Food can drastically affect how you feel on a daily basis. If you're wanting to find balance in this area, I suggest that you work to follow a healthy lifestyle that is sustainable for you, rather than an extreme program. Find a system that works best for your season of life and your family dynamic but take control of this essential area in your life. As far as it depends on you, put the best possible fuel into your body so that you can go the distance.

Fuel your body to go the distance.

C. Rest

Psalm 127:2 NIV "In vain you rise early and stay up late toiling for food to eat—for he grants sleep to those he loves."

My two favorite times of the day are early morning when everything is still quiet and getting into bed after a long day. If I had my way, I could easily go to bed as early as eight o'clock. This rarely happens, but my husband and I have realized that we are on very different sleep schedules. His favorite and most clear-thinking time is late at night, whereas mine is in the early hours of the morning. If we worked only according to this, neither of us would get much sleep! Because only one of us is a night owl, we have learned to be considerate of one another. I do not demand that Greg comes to bed at the same time as me, and he doesn't expect me to wait up as late as he does. There are times when he will work in bed while I go to sleep, and sometimes I will stay up and we will work or watch a movie together. If the afternoon allows, I will take a short power nap so that I can do this easily.

No matter our preferences, we both have to discipline ourselves to make sure we get adequate sleep that enables us to stay healthy and alert in what God has called us to do. The question is, "How much is enough?"

We are all unique and some need less sleep than others, but a lifestyle of sleep deprivation will eventually affect our health and ability to function at our best. Lack of good sleep should be an exception not a lifestyle.

Lack of good sleep should be an exception not a lifestyle.

There are a number of factors that can affect our sleep patterns negatively such as hormonal changes, worry and mental stress, certain foods, our environment etc. I personally went through a season of exhaustion because of broken sleep patterns. If this is your reality, I would suggest you ask trusted friends to pray for you and consider speaking to a doctor or someone who can help you with restored sleep.

Good, restorative sleep plays a vital role in keeping us emotionally stable; this is key for us as leaders. We pay a high price when we mistreat those we lead and say things we regret due to exhaustion and irritability. For the sake of those we lead, it is important to pursue a lifestyle of adequate rest.

Reflection

1. How can you prioritize your physical health in the area of fitness? What habits might work best for your season and lifestyle?

2. What has worked well for you in maintaining a level of healthy nutrition? What has been a struggle? Do some research or speak to people that can help you in this area if necessary.

3. Does your lifestyle allow for adequate sleep? Is there anything hindering your sleep patterns and what can you do to change this?

Remember . . .

Pursuing physical wellness enhances your ability to accomplish your purpose.

Lack of good sleep should be an exception not a lifestyle.

Rest is a gift from God, enjoy it.

5

There's always one more thing

Time Management

If we don't manage our time, others will. There will always be one more thing to do, one more person to call, or one more meeting to attend. Too many leaders are exhausted because they feel obliged to say yes to each need and event. Often these responses are rooted in guilt, not wanting to disappoint or hurt someone's feelings. Insecurity will cause us to say yes to things that the Lord is not necessarily requiring of us in a given season. If we are involved in everything, we feel important. Leading from any of these places cannot last, and eventually we will be too exhausted to attend or lead anything.

We do ourselves and those we lead a great disservice when we don't manage our time responsibly.

Take time and ask the Lord and trusted voices in your life what you are called to do in this particular season and what responsibilities you might have taken on that are not yours to carry. This is always a helpful and freeing exercise that I do a few times a year.

We all have the gift of twenty-four hours a day to manage. Efficient time management will require discipline and putting systems in place. There will always be other things to give our time and attention to, and if we do not have a plan up front, these things will absorb us. What has been helpful to me is to plan my week ahead and have specific days and times that I give to the assignments God is giving me to do. As far as it depends on me, I stick to this. It is helpful to let those close to you know what your general schedule is so that people understand when you're not able to attend a given social function.

Identify the main goals that you need to accomplish and set a time for those to be done. According to those goals, make a list of what it will take to accomplish them. These need to be doable given our individual lifestyles, and they need to be measurable. Setting huge goals or New Year's resolutions without a plan just brings frustration and often failure.

I like structure and lists, so I often start my day with a list of things I need to accomplish based on the goals I have set. I try to complete the most important things first. There are times when I need to close my office door and switch my phone off for a few hours because I'm giving my attention to what He is requiring of me. Most other things can wait! Once we are sure of what our priorities are, it is easier to say no to good things that are not where we need to be giving our energy.

Reflection

1. What responsibilities have you taken on at this time that might not be necessary or are weighing you down?

2. What system has worked well for your personality to help you accomplish your goals? Are there areas where you might need a different system? Work with a trusted friend or mentor if necessary, to help you with this.

Remember . . .

Insecurity will push you to say yes to things that the Lord is not requiring of you.

You are responsible to manage your time.

6

Do not disturb

Making appointments with yourself

"Solitude is a chosen separation for refining your soul. Isolation is what you crave when you neglect the first" Wayne Cordeiro (author of Leading on Empty: Refilling your tank and renewing your passion)

I have learned to make what I call 'me' appointments. If I don't schedule these, they will seldom happen. Over and above my morning devotion, I need time alone to read, go for a walk or page through a magazine with a cup of tea. These don't have to be long, but they are necessary for me to take a breath and lay aside other demands. The needs will still be there in half an hour, but I will be in a better frame of mind to deal with them. Never feel guilty for taking time to refresh your soul.

Everybody benefits when the leader is refreshed, and everybody suffers when the leader has nothing more to give.

Everybody benefits when the leader is refreshed, and everybody suffers when the leader has nothing more to give.

Everybody benefits when the leader is refreshed, and everybody suffers when the leader has nothing more to give.

Everyone that is in your sphere, including your family, will benefit greatly from these times. Recently a young mom asked me, "But what will suffer if I take this time?" Nothing. In fact, those you love most will eventually suffer if you lead from an emotionally depleted place. A friend of mine who has three children under the age of nine has a two-hour time of rest each afternoon where her children are required to stay in their bedrooms and read and play. The youngest one still naps. This is a necessary time not only for the children but also for her as a mom. Whether you're leading a ministry or team in a corporate environment or you're a mom leading her children at home, we all need moments of quiet and solitude.

It is vital to plan these times ahead. If you don't, they will probably not happen because life is busy and there is always the next thing to do. According to our personalities, some will perceive a need for this more than others, but I do believe we all benefit from time alone when we can switch off mentally from our demands. Give yourself permission to not be on for a short time each day and give your mind time to rest and replenish without distractions.

This time will look different according to where we are in our lives. It might mean locking the bathroom door and asking your husband to watch the children while you enjoy a bubble bath or finding a coffee shop close to your office where you can take a short break alone. Figure out what works for you but make time for solitude so that you never get to a place of craving isolation out of desperation. Even Jesus made a plan to take time alone, away from the crowds as he told His disciples to have a boat ready. The boat would take Him to a quiet place to replenish His soul.

> Mark 3:9-10 MSG "He told His disciples to get a boat ready so he wouldn't be trampled by the crowd. He had healed many people, and now everyone who had something wrong was pushing and shoving to get near and touch him"

Wise leaders make a plan for solitude.

Wise leaders make sure they have a boat ready! Make a plan for solitude.

Reflection

1. We need to give ourselves permission to take regular breaks. What does this look like for you?

2. What needs to happen for you to have this time?

3. Make a plan for this to be part of your schedule, as everyone around you will benefit.

Remember . . .

Everyone benefits when the leader is refreshed. Everyone suffers when the leader has nothing more to give.

Never feel guilty for taking time to refresh your soul.

Wise leaders make sure they have a plan for solitude.

7

Limiting My Yes

Prioritizing essentials and setting boundaries

A younger me used to be horrified when I'd see more seasoned leaders saying no to others. "What hard hearts you have!" I'd think, "Where's the love? Because Jesus lives in me, I can do anything, and take on any need or challenge! Who needs boundaries when we have a world to save?"

Over the years, I have grown wiser and realized that even Jesus had boundaries when He ministered to people.

Jesus would wipe the dust from His feet and move on if they didn't receive Him. He would withdraw to lonely places to connect with His Father.

Mark 6:31 NIV Jesus says, "Come with me by yourselves to a quiet place and get some rest."

Many were coming and going, and they needed to eat and rest amidst so much output. Jesus, being a wise leader, knew this.

There is nothing noble about burning out for Jesus.

There is nothing noble about burning out for Jesus. Amidst our zeal to walk in all that He has for us, we need to find places of rest and refreshing. Just like a page has margin so that the words don't fall off the edge, our lives need margin too.

Healthy boundaries, both in relationships and schedules, will ensure we go the distance and enjoy what the Lord has called us to do.

If you are a leader in any capacity, whether it be in your home as a parent, in your church or business, you have multiple demands on your time and energy. People find safety and counsel, as they should from you, but there needs to be a limit to your yes.

I have found it helpful to figure out the big rocks and to place these on my calendar first. The value of my relationship with my Lord, my spouse, my children and grandchildren, close friends and those I minister with in team needs to be reflected on my calendar.

Once I know these relationships will not be neglected due to busyness, I can add other things as the Lord leads. I have learned not to take my calendar out at church (nothing like some dear heart leaning over and seeing an empty space!). It has worked best for me to get back to people once I have established my schedule for the week and put those big rocks in place first. Find out what works well for you personally inside the boundaries that you set for your life.

If we are going to be effective leaders, our first responsibility is to lead ourselves well.

Our first responsibility is to lead ourselves well.

Our first response is to the Lord's call and what He is requiring of us. Through this lens we set boundaries and healthy margin in our lives so that we minister from a place of stability and strength and not from a place of burnout because we didn't attend to our own souls or take time to hear His voice.

A key question to ask is, "In this situation, what are you requiring of me, Lord?" He will always be faithful to supply us with what we need to give. It's in the secret place that many times the Lord will give me clarity as to what I need to do or not do. Peace comes when we respond to His voice.

John 10:27 NIV "My sheep listen to my voice; I know them, and they follow me."

In his book, Leading on Empty: Refilling your tank and Renewing your mind, Wayne Cordeiro writes about the importance of distinguishing between a concern and a responsibility. There will always be situations to be concerned about and pray about and our hearts will go out to those in need. Not every need is ours to personally meet. That would be impossible. We can put people in touch with others or even make suggestions, but we cannot personally solve every problem. I have found this distinction helpful when facing multiple demands. Asking the Lord and filtering these through the lens of what He is asking of me in a certain season has enabled me to respond with genuine concern or take responsibility for what needs to be done.

Reflection

1. Take a few minutes and ask the Lord what He has on His heart for you in your particular season.

2. List your key relationships and prioritize time with them above others.

Remember . . .

There is nothing noble about burning out for Jesus.

Effective leaders take responsibility to first lead themselves.

PART 2
Strong Foundations

A building is only as strong as its foundations. Strong foundations are necessary to hold a structure in place and ensure the safety of the occupants when adverse weather such as storms or earthquakes arise. The taller the building, the deeper the foundation needs to be. The same principle of strong foundations applies to our lives and whatever we have been called to build.

I'm writing in the context of a healthy marriage being foundational in ministry. I am not saying that single people do not have a strong foundation. Our foundation is primarily in the Lord. If you're reading this as a leader who is not married, I believe your foundation is the strength of your walk with the Lord and being in submission to a healthy leadership team who encourage you, protect you, and make space for you.

8

Covenant comes First

Building a strong marriage

When Greg and I started dating, we were in our senior year of high school and as deeply in love as one can be at the tender age of eighteen. When we graduated, Greg enlisted in the military for two years, and I started my four-year education degree. Two years later, Greg responded to a clear call from the Lord to full time ministry in the church and pursued his own educational journey at a Bible college. During this time, we ended our relationship to take time to pray and seek God as to whether we were to be married. Four months later, after much prayer and many tears (from me), we both felt like we had heard from the Lord that we were to be married. As tough as those months were, our marriage is built on a clear word from the Lord which has been an anchor for us throughout the years.

I believe any solid ministry, if led by a married person or couple, is validated by a marriage that is grounded on the word of God and is an example of what the Lord intends marriage to be.

Sadly, there are too many stories of ministry marriages that fail due to overwhelming pressure, or spouses who neglect each other and find attention elsewhere.

Our greatest allegiance is to our two primary covenants, one with the Lord and one with our spouse. These take precedence over our ministry, our business, our children, or any other relationship.

Our covenantal relationship with God and our spouse comes first.

Taking care of our covenantal relationships first is vital as they set a solid foundation for everything else we do.

If you're married, schedule regular times for you as a couple. Take time to have fun and build your friendship from the very beginning. If you have small children, make sure you have dates that are just for the two of you. Your children need to see you investing in your marriage, because you want them to do the same one day. Children need to understand that mom and dad need time on their own. It is healthy for them to see you go away and know that you will come back. We are doing our children a great favor when we give them the gift of parents who love each other. We also pay them a huge disservice when we don't intentionally build into what gives them great security. A commonly believed myth is that it's not fair or it's not a good season for us to be away from our children for any given amount of time.

The truth is that when we are diligent to build into our marriages, we are giving our children more security rather than less attention. A day will come when your children will grow up and leave home and then it will be just the two of you. This can be a wonderful time of freedom, as you're not managing school schedules or running carpools. It can also be a very lonely and somewhat scary time if you find yourself at home with a stranger who you have not connected with for years. It's never too late to find reconciliation, as God is a restorer, but set things in place so that the latter years are the best years.

We have found it helpful to be deliberate about having at least one night a week at home without an agenda.

We are responsible to fight for our marriages.

As leaders, we are responsible to fight for our marriages and set them as our highest priority next to our relationship with the Lord. It is helpful and inspiring to surround ourselves with couples who have strong marriages and who love one another deeply. Do not neglect sexual intimacy with your spouse. You're the only legitimate lover they can have, so be the best you can. Read books, do a marriage course or anything that will help you keep this area of your marriage healthy and frequent. I know well how the pressures and demands of life can distract us, but we are the only ones who can fight for our marriages. Make time to pray together regularly. Our prayers of agreement have great power to affect what God has declared over our lives. We partner in prayer to hear His voice and declare His truth.

Periodically, we will carve out time to talk about and assess how we both feel we are doing in the following areas of our marriage:

1. Sexually

Are we both satisfied and enjoying love making? Would we benefit from reading a book or going on a marriage retreat?

2. Spiritually

How is our prayer life doing together? What is the Lord saying to each one?

3. Friendship

Amidst the busyness, are we enjoying our friendship and making time to just be together?

4. Communication

Do we both feel heard and understood? How is our conflict resolution?

5. Fun

Having fun together is a high priority for us, but we have to be deliberate about making time for it. How are we adding fun to our marriage?

Whether you are reading this from a place of great strength or from a place of pain in your marriage, I would like to suggest that you take a few minutes somewhere uninterrupted and ask the Lord to show you how He sees your spouse. When we view people through God's eyes, it will change how we relate and pray for them. Let me remind you that our Father in heaven is a redeemer by nature and if you ask Him, He will come alongside and redeem anything that's been wounded and bring wholeness and healing. We have witnessed many marriages, including ministry marriages that looked almost hopeless, be magnificently restored because of His great power.

We can only impart to others what we ourselves have. If we are going to be leaders who impart healing and wholeness, we have to minister from our own firm foundation. God's intent is for us to enjoy all the beauty and satisfaction and joy that comes from a marriage built on the firm foundation of Jesus Christ and His word.

Reflection

1. How do you as a couple make time to build into your marriage?

2. Consider planning a time when you can talk about how you both feel you are doing in the following areas of your marriage:

   a. Sexually

   b. Spiritually

   c. Friendship

   d. Communication

   e. Fun

Remember . . .

Your covenantal relationships with God and with your spouse come first.

When you are diligent to build into your marriage, you are giving your children more security rather than less attention.

You are the only legitimate lover your spouse can have, so be the best you can.

9

Everyone In

Parenting and Ministry

When our daughter Nicole was young, she would go to ballet lessons on Monday afternoon, which she looked forward to each week. Monday was also our day off, so we had a fun tradition. Greg and I would pick her up from ballet and head to the beach to meet close friends of ours who had children of similar age. We spent most Monday evenings eating burgers at a favorite restaurant and watching our children enjoy the sand and sea. There wasn't much that could deter us from this; it was a top priority to have fun and build memories as a family.

As a leader in any capacity, there will be a fair demand on our time. I believe it is our responsibility to make our children (our first disciples) know that they are our first priority above the needs of others.

Our children need to see us protect regular, designated family time.

Our children need to experience regular, designated family time. They need to hear us saying no to the needs of others at times or see us not taking a call because we have a date with them and as a family. In ministry families, too many children grow up with a negative view of church because they have felt like there was no time for them. There will be plenty of opportunity for them to realize that they do need to share your attention with others since that is what you have been called to as a family. (This can be a call to the church, to business, education etc)

We believe God calls families. He has a destiny and purpose for you as an individual and as a family. We equip our children for their part in the family call when we share with them what the Lord is saying and take time to tell them stories of His provision and goodness. When our daughter was younger, we would tell her that we were trusting the Lord for provision in an area. We would include her as we prayed about this and when these prayers were answered, we would give thanks as a family. These were teaching moments that settled in her that God is our provider.

We spent six years leading a church in South Africa when the Lord spoke to us about relocating to Atlanta, Georgia, to start Northlands Church. This was a three-year process of praying together as a family and transitioning the church so we could leave well. Our daughter was very much a part of this process. We were all counting the cost of leaving what was familiar and comfortable and stepping into something new and unknown. We were leaving friends and family because we knew we had heard from the Lord to move and start a church in Atlanta. We explained to Nicole from a young age that we were called to minister as a family, and that each of us would have to sacrifice something in order to gain the greater thing that the Lord had for us. Just as we had to leave our families and beloved church community, she also had to leave behind her sweet circle of friends and family. From a young age, she knew we are a family who responds to God's voice, no matter the cost.

> Psalm 78:4 NIV We will not hide them from their descendants; we will tell the next generation the praiseworthy deeds of the Lord, his power, and the wonders he has done. 5 He decreed statutes for Jacob and established the law in Israel, which he commanded our ancestors to teach their children,6 so the next generation would know them, even the children yet to be born, and they in turn would tell their children. 7 Then they would put their trust in God and would not forget his deeds but would keep his commands.

I believe God calls families to serve Him together and it's our responsibility to communicate this practically to our children. As they become adults, they will make their own choices, but we can certainly set their sails in the right direction. Include your children as you pray for specific things and be deliberate about thanking them for sacrifices of time that they make. Leaders children are often the first to arrive and the last to leave. Remind them of the joy and privilege of serving the King and His Kingdom. When we parent our children and include them in what we are called to, we can help them embrace all that the Lord has for them rather than hinder them by allowing a negative perspective of what should be a great joy.

Matthew 19:14 NIV "Jesus said, "Let the little children come to me, and do not hinder them, for the kingdom of heaven belongs to such as these.""

Any vocation that requires being intricately involved in people's lives and emotions is never going to fit a nine to five schedule. I have worked as a teacher in a school that has specific work hours and been in ministry in the church for over thirty years and both of these can easily be 24/7. It's not easy to emotionally switch off when you are confronted with people's pain and deep needs. I remember meeting a lady for coffee who had ongoing health issues and a troubled marriage. I knew our time together would be focused on this, and I felt quite helpless. As clearly as I know His voice, the Holy Spirit whispered to me, "It is not your job to heal her." My role at that moment was to love her and pray for her but not take on responsibility to the solve the issues at hand. The Lord has commanded us to lay hands on the sick, but we cannot take on the full weight of every need. That is His to do.

I have come to realize that ministry is not a job, it's a lifestyle and a calling. Many times, it will be unpredictable and inconvenient. It will mess with our well-organized day because crises don't wait for the perfect moment. I often get asked the question, "So what does your week usually look like?" Or "What is a typical day for you?" There is seldom a "typical" in ministry. As much as I rely on schedules, I know I have not signed up for a nine-to-five lifestyle! Each day, each week will come with its own surprises and situations that will demand our flexibility and that of our families.

Having said that, I also know that to maintain a healthy marriage, which is foundational for ministry and family, boundaries are essential. It is vital to build margin that allows emotional replenishment and mental breaks.

It can be as simple as taking a day off and not being readily available to every call. It means scheduling times away as a couple and as a family. Remember, we are modeling for our children what we wish for them as they grow up and have families of their own.

Years ago, a more seasoned ministry couple told us they would not be available to take any calls while on vacation and that they hoped they would not meet anyone who knew them. I remember being shocked and a little disgusted at this! "How can they say they love people and think like this?" Thirty years and two churches later, I understand.

Boundaries are absolutely necessary if we are going to thrive, love deeply, and finish strong.

Boundaries allow us to thrive, love deeply, and finish strong. Something that has been helpful to us through the years is to make sure we have one meal together as a family each day. For us that was dinner time. This was a time to connect with each other and not answer phone calls or reply to text messages but to focus on the people around the table. Try this in your home, just one meal or moment in the day to be together. Take time to ask about each one's day, laugh at the funny things that might have happened and pray for each other as it fits naturally into this time. Times of connection will look different according to our different family dynamics but let's make sure they happen.

When we plan our week, we try to make sure that we are not out every night. It's amazing how quickly my calendar can get filled up if I don't block off times ahead. An appointment at home with our children or spouse is just as valuable as our time with friends and those we lead. Sometimes, a quiet evening and a walk after dinner is the most spiritual thing we can do!

Keeping our marriages and families strong plays a large part in keeping our callings strong. Of course, as our children grow up they will make their own lifestyle choices for which we are not responsible. We pray they make wise ones as we set good, healthy examples for them to follow.

If you still have children under your care, they are your first disciples. Make sure they get the best of you and that your spouse doesn't have to settle for an over-extended, worn-out partner because you have poured all you have into others. Build in the margin and build in the boundaries as you model kingdom life for them. Teach them, as you sit around the table, what it means to make decisions according to what the Lord has said to you as a family. Let them know that they are very much part of what God has called you to. This means there will be certain privileges for them as well as sacrifices. Thank them for what they do so that you can do what you do. Help them to joyfully serve the Lord as they understand the why of what happens in your family.

Reflection

1. If you have children at home, ask the Lord to show you how to communicate with them that God has called you as a family. Make time to thank them for what they do.

2. Plan a fun outing as a family.

3. Are there areas in your life where more boundaries are needed to give you more time with your spouse and children?

Remember . . .

God calls families to serve Him together.

At times your children need to hear you say no to others so that you can say yes to them.

Boundaries allow us to thrive, love deeply, and finish strong.

10

Come rest a while

Home as a Haven

As much as our homes are a tool for the task that God has given us to love people and a place where we practice hospitality, they are also meant to be a haven of rest where we can unstring the proverbial bow and let our guards down. Our homes should be places of peace where the family can shut the world out and focus on one another. When our homes are a haven for us, they become a haven for all who come through our doors.

There are times when it's okay to say no to those who might want to stop by for a visit, because at this moment our home is a haven of rest for our family. In our own lives, Sunday afternoons are our time to relax after a full weekend.

Typically, my husband likes to kick his shoes off, get comfortable on the sofa and watch football. I love a Sunday afternoon nap and a long walk if the weather permits.

If at all possible, we guard this time closely. We need this time of rest after a wonderful morning with the people God has entrusted to us to love and lead.

In my early years of ministry, I would feel guilty doing this. Just doing nothing felt like a waste of time! No! Times like these are essential and very spiritual!

The people we lead benefit greatly when we make sure we are refreshed.

If you have children living at home, their lives are no doubt filled with multiple fun activities and school commitments. There are times when we have to make sure that we orchestrate times of rest for our children that do not include friends and outside activities. (They will likely not recognize their need for this at the time).

As much as our homes are a place of comfort for those we lead, let's ensure that they are also a place of rest and respite for ourselves and our family. There truly is no place like home when we get this right.

Reflection

1. How is your home a haven to you and your family?

2. What will be helpful to enhance this?

Remember . . .

Your home is meant to be a haven for your rest.

Your home can be a place of comfort for those you lead, but not

before it is a place of respite for your family.

11

Southern Hospitality

Home as a tool for the task

Growing up, I was exposed to many formal dinners because my dad was a diplomat in the South African Embassy in Brussels and Paris. Some of these we attended as a family, and as young girls my sister and I loved getting all dressed up in our formal dresses and patent leather shoes. My parents hosted some of these occasions at our home, and we were trained how to serve food from the right and take one plate at a time from the left. Over the years, we helped serve at many of our parent's dinner parties and watched as beautiful platters were prepared and presented. My sister and I loved sampling the delicious food and watching my mom add the final touches to make sure everything looked just perfect. Her beautiful gift of hospitality was a huge asset to her role in this season. Our home was a haven for others who were acclimating to a new culture, and because my mom has always been a gracious hostess and excellent cook, we learned the value of hospitality from a young age.

When we moved to Atlanta, we got to experience wonderful southern hospitality. I truly think it must be some of the best in the world. Whether you're walking in the street or being served at a restaurant, everyone is so polite and warm. The Bible also holds hospitality as a high value.

We are told to practice hospitality and to be hospitable to one another (Romans 12:13 & 1 Peter 4:9). Our homes are tools for the task of loving the people God has given us and a place where we practice hospitality.

Hospitality is important enough to the Lord that it is listed as one of the grace gifts in Romans 12. He loves it when we love people well. This includes setting an atmosphere that is warm and welcoming and a safe place for those who cross our threshold. God has given us authority to set the spiritual tone or atmosphere in our homes.

We have authority to speak His peace and rest into our homes.

We have authority to speak His peace and rest into our homes and to disallow contention and strife. Decide what you want people to walk into when they arrive at your door. We know it's not always going to be perfect, and yes, there will be times of tension in a family (even in the pastor's home!), but we can make a choice to not allow those moments to rule. We can choose to be a family of peace and a place where others find rest and healing.

Years ago, while on staff at another church, one of the leaders said to me, "If it's easy, you will do it again." We know that not everything is meant to be easy but having a plan that works certainly helps!

Because our home is a tool in the Lord's hands and a place where we entertain fairly often, it has been helpful to me to have a few things that I know work well to create a warm and inviting atmosphere. I'm sure you have things that work well for you as well. Here are some of mine:

I always have a box of votive candles on hand as candles seem to make the simplest setting feel warm and inviting. My personal favorite is a vase of fresh flowers. Sometimes it's a small vase with a few flowers picked from the yard. Other times it can be more elaborate arrangement depending on the occasion. Anything fresh works for me! Music can play a part in creating an environment, so we usually have soft background music playing in our home.

When it comes to preparing meals for guests, I have found it practical and stress-free to master three or four meals from start to finish that I know work well. This has given me a confidence in entertaining because it no longer requires much thought and gives me the freedom to enjoy my guests, without worrying whether the food turned out okay! You might be someone who loves to try new recipes when entertaining so this might sound boring to you. Again, whatever we do has to work well for us so that we will want to do it again.

Where possible I like to plan two nights in a row of having people for dinner. This makes it easy for me, since my flowers are already done, and my house is already clean. If your family doesn't mind, you can even double up on the meal so that you only cook once.

The atmosphere in our homes and the warmth with which we receive guests will have a much greater impact than the meal we serve. We have enjoyed fine dining around a beautifully set table, and we have enjoyed pizza while sitting on boxes helping friends move. Both have been enjoyable and life giving because of the hospitality of the hosts.

> Romans 12:13 NIV "Share with the Lord's people who are in need. Practice hospitality."

Reflection Time

1. List a few homes where you have felt most comfortable and at ease. What in particular allowed for this?

2. How do you use your home as a tool for the task?

Remember . . .

Your home can be a tool for the task of ministry.

You have authority to declare peace in your home.

Part 3

Relationships

From the beginning of time, God made it clear that He created us for connection when He said in Genesis chapter 1, "It is not good for man to be alone." His motivation for sending His son was love, as the Bible says, "For God so LOVED the world that He gave His only son." Throughout the scriptures, we are told to love, encourage, build up, and to forgive. None of this would be necessary if we weren't designed to be in relationship with other people. We were never meant to live isolated from authentic relationship.

12

Created for connection

The importance of Friendship

Having authentic friendships is not only something I enjoy but something I need and value. Being a leader in a church context requires me to connect with many people at varying levels. If you are part of a growing organization, you will understand that you cannot be close friends with each one. My personal frustration is that there are so many wonderful people and not enough of me to hear every story! Understanding relationships and my responsibility in them has helped me balance my time and manage these frustrations well.

Levels of relationships

Ezekiel 47:10 speaks about fish of many kinds. This aptly describes the people and relationships we will have as we love and lead. We should expect and be prepared for many different types of

---

relationships and people. It has been helpful for me, where possible, to identify these relationships and the part they play in my life.

We are called to love everyone, but we are not called to have the same level of relationship with everyone. Not only is this humanly impossible, it is also modeled very clearly by Jesus Himself.

Let's look a little more closely at the model of Jesus' relationships.

Jesus had His 3, His 12, and the crowds

Jesus' three closest friends were Peter, James, and John. They were part of His inner circle. These men were with Jesus when He raised the synagogue ruler's daughter from the dead, and they stayed with Him in His time of deep sorrow in the garden of Gethsemane. It is also said that Jesus stayed in Peter's home.

It was John who leaned against His chest at the last supper and was told by Jesus that Judas was the betrayer. John was at the cross when Jesus died and was commissioned by Jesus to take care of His mother, Mary.

In Matthew 16:18 Peter is affirmed by Jesus as the rock on which He will build His church, a key role in the Kingdom.

James was Jesus's brother, and along with Peter and John, witnessed miracles that the other disciples didn't. He took Peter, James, and John with Him up the mount of Transfiguration.

His twelve were Simon-Peter, Andrew, James son of Zebedee, John, Philip, Bartholomew, Thomas, Simon the zealot, Matthew, James, son of Alpheus, Thaddeus, and Judas Iscariot, who was replaced by Matthias in Acts 1:20-26.

These twelve went with Jesus, and He mentored them. He taught them the things of the Kingdom, expecting them to go out and do the things they had learned from their Master.

The crowds were those who followed Jesus from town to town, or those who witnessed the miracles He performed as He went from place to place. They heard His teachings and went away encouraged and healed.

Jesus loved all these people enough to go to the cross for them, but He didn't share is heart with all of them or give equal amount of time to them.

Identify your different levels of relationships.

It has been helpful to me to identify different levels of relationships as well as what these relationships and friendships bring to my life. Each one is a gift from the Lord to either strengthen me or to be strengthened and launched into their God-given purpose. It's a worthwhile exercise to identify your 3 (confidantes & close friends), your 12 (friends), and the crowd (work colleagues and acquaintances).

The give and take in relationships

Being able to identify the nature of different relationships in my life has been most helpful, both in relating to the person as well as managing my expectations of that person.

Most of us will at some stage know the frustration and even heartache of unmet expectations when it comes to our relationships.

All relationships add or detract from us. Identifying these different types of relationships will help us set boundaries, have realistic expectations, and glean the most from people who will strengthen us personally.

In my life, I've identified six types of relationships:

1. Mentors

A hallmark of maturity in a leader is the purposeful pursuit of mentorship. This can happen through reading, listening to teachings and spending time with people who champion us and who will speak truthfully into our lives. No matter how far up the leadership ladder we may be, we never reach a place where we cannot learn from someone ahead of us. It is a dangerous place to be when we believe we no longer need others to teach us. Identify a few people that have inspired you and strengthened you to be a better and more skilled leader. If possible, spend time with these people or listen regularly to their material.

Read books that sharpen you and develop you in your God-given calling. Keep learning, and you will be a leader that many will want to follow.

2. Builders

It's a good habit to figure out who in your current circle is passionate about the same things you are. If you have shared a truth, these friends can't wait to get together and add their perspective or share what they have heard with others. They take notes and will repeat what you have taught. These are your cheerleaders and those who stoke the fires of your calling. Within this group will be those who are loyal behind your back. I like to call these the builders. They will work alongside to build what the Lord has put in your heart. Identify your builders.

Nehemiah 2:18 AMPC "Let us rise up and build! So they strengthened their hands for the good work"

3. Disciples

Jesus set a clear example for us to disciple and send out. Who is the Lord placing in your sphere to teach what you know so that what you do can be multiplied?

Who are those younger than you who can run further and stand on your shoulders? We have a responsibility to raise up the next generation of leaders and influencers. At times we will need to trust those that might not have the same level of experience, and yet God has given them to us to mentor and release. We will speak a little more on this very vital topic of raising up next generation leaders in a later chapter.

4. Spectators

In every community, there will people who are just happy to be there and sit in the back row. They will occasionally attend events and sometimes offer their help, but they are not going to be people you can lean on. As leaders who intuitively see needs and opportunities to get things done, this group can add a level of frustration. I have learned not to expect of people what they are not able or willing to give. For example, if someone is struggling with depression, they may not be able to invest much emotional energy into a friendship. Sometimes people don't have confidence in themselves and do not believe they have anything of value to bring.

We are commanded to love all, not lean on all.

We are commanded in scripture to love all, not lean on all. As we continue to speak life over them, we will also find great joy when those from this group come to a realization that they have a vital part to play and step into that.

5. Broken

I cannot expect close friendships from those who don't have much to give. I need to recognize that my role is to minister God's love and healing to those I lead.

At times, these interactions can be quite draining emotionally. Even Jesus acknowledged that He felt power go from Him when He ministered to the woman with the issue of blood.

Guard your own heart and time when ministering to the broken. Jesus withdrew often to be with His Father because He spent much time administering healing and deliverance and recognized His need to be refreshed. May we do the same so that we can be effective ministers and see many broken and hurting people come to wholeness.

6. Critics

As leaders who are called to watch over those whom the Lord brings, we do have a responsibility to identify those who come in to cause disunity and who pull against the very thing we are building. These people often appoint themselves as policemen who will want to constantly "make you aware" of what is not working or what will definitely not succeed.

The ones with a leadership gift who draw others to themselves pose a greater threat. I do not find any joy in confrontational conversations, but there have been times when I have had to have the tough talks and put an end to what is potentially destructive. We have used a bus analogy: this bus (our church, in our case) is going here (our vision). If you want to go in a different direction, then maybe it's time to ring the bell and get off and find another bus. You can no longer sit at the back and shout directions. Your role is not to drive this bus (i.e lead this vision). This is never pleasant, but it comes with the leadership hat.

When the enemy tried to manipulate Nehemiah and cause him to come down from what he was building, he refused. Be aware of the distractions and deal with them as gently and as clearly as possible.

> Nehemiah 6:2 NIV Sanballat and Geshem sent me this message: "Come, let us meet together in one of the villages on the plain of Ono." But they were scheming to harm me; 3 so I sent messengers to them with this reply: "I am carrying on a great project and cannot go down. Why should the work stop while I leave it and go down to you?" 4 Four times they sent me the same message, and each time I gave them the same answer.

Reflection

1. Using the 3, 12 & crowds model mentioned at the beginning of the chapter, who are your 3, 12 and crowd?

2. Identify people in your own life in each of the six mentioned categories.

3. Are there distractions in your life that are causing you to "come down from the wall" you are called to build?

Remember . . .

The great commandment is to love all, not lean on all.

Jesus had relationships in different circles, and He withdrew often.

He invites us to follow His example.

13

Heart Healthy

Living un-offended

My heart is racing as I'm about to have a difficult conversation. The atmosphere in the room is quiet because we both know this is not going to be a comfortable meeting. I personally love speaking life over people and encouraging them with what the Lord says about them. I love telling them of the Father's great love and that He has good things for them.

If I had my selfish way, I would avoid all meetings where correction and rebuke are called for. I play these meetings out way too many times in my head before they happen. I would say this is my least favorite part of leadership, but it's part of what we sign up for.

So why do I mention all this as regards to a healthy heart? I have found that these tough conversations can also be a seed bed for offense and hurt and rejection for both parties. It's in these moments where people have reacted with sharp and hurtful comments attacking our leadership and saying things that are simply not true but certainly cause pain. I have had to guard my heart and not allow these words to stick.

The scriptures tell us to guard our hearts above all things because from them flows everything we do. I've seen too many wounded leaders leave their post and harden their hearts because they did not heed this advice. If you open a wound, poison comes out. It has very little to do with you personally. You are just the target at the time. Most people will ultimately see your motive and hopefully receive the correction that will be most valuable to them. If this does not happen, we have to be able to walk away, knowing we did what is required of us as leaders. Nobody said it would be easy, but oh the joy when we get to partner with the Lord to see His Bride walk in freedom!

Proverbs 4:23 NIV "Above all else guard your heart, for everything you do flows from it "

Proverbs 15:13 NIV "A happy heart makes the face cheerful, but heartache crushes the spirit."

Loving and leading people is a privilege. Many times, we have wrestled in prayer to see some awesome breakthroughs. We have been the voice of comfort on the other end of the phone. We have spoken life and peace into situations of great pain and turmoil. Added to this, there are times when we will need to be a voice of correction or rebuke because those whom we love are not aligning their lives or decisions with their true identity in Christ. As responsible leaders, there will be times when it is necessary to have the tough conversations because we care too much to avoid them (see Chapter 9).

Everyday opportunities of offense will present themselves to us. Admittedly, I have accepted some of these invitations only to find that they have worn me down and distracted me from hearing the good things the Lord has for me. Proverbs 19:11 counsels us to overlook an offense.

Offense is inevitable! What we do with it is key to our well-being and keeping our hearts healthy.

Offense is inevitable! What we do with it is key to our well-being and keeping our hearts healthy. We cannot afford to harbor offense.

Sometimes a word will be spoken, or actions taken to deliberately hurt, but most often it will not be intentional or with evil motive!

It will most likely be from immature, thoughtless or self-centered behavior that none the less does affect us. For example, if someone forgets an appointment more than once or consistently arrives late to meet with you, you have an opportunity to be offended because, "clearly they have no regard for my time or how busy I am."

The reality is that they probably just have too much on their plate and it has nothing to do with how they feel about you personally. This is a mild example, but when we recognize that we have been offended, we have to make a choice to walk in forgiveness. We get to choose whether what has been positioned against us will dislodge us from our peace and joy or strengthen us, as we trust the Lord and hand these offenses to Him. In the course of our lives, there will be many situations that will have potential to cause offense and distract us from the goodness of God. We cannot afford this.

We cannot afford to harbor offense.

There are attitudes and actions that others may choose to adopt that we as leaders simply cannot afford.

When I feel I have been wronged, misquoted or just plain hurt, the temptation to call and tell someone how awful that person was or how they twisted a story has certainly been there! These are the times when we have to stand alone, because God has called us to lead and we do not have the luxury of entering into gossip. There's too much to do to advance the Kingdom! I have a dear friend who would say, "It's okay to go home and have a good cry and then move on." There will be many opportunities to get our feelings hurt. What we do with these situations will affect our walk with the Lord and those we lead negatively or positively. We get to choose. The Bible tells us clearly to forgive as we have been forgiven.

When I have offended someone

Ephesians 4:32 NIV "Be kind and compassionate to one another, forgiving each other, just as in Christ God forgave you."

If you have been in leadership for any amount of time, you have had people come to you because they have had their feelings hurt by something you said or did. Many times, you are not aware until you are told. Here are some of mine:

"You walked past me twice on Sunday and never greeted me."

"I wasn't invited to an event. "

"Why was Jane asked to speak and I wasn't? "

"Why have you not accepted my friend request on Facebook?"

"I don't understand why I haven't been asked to lead?"

"How come you get to speak more than anyone else?"

As you read these, you might well be chuckling in disbelief, but the reality to that person is that they have been overlooked by someone who they trust as their leader. More than likely, hll as I will share towards the end of the book.

Whether justified or not, feelings have been hurt and as leaders this is a good opportunity to lead with humility and just say, "I'm so sorry this offended you, I had no intention of hurting you." Though the circumstances might not change, let them know that you value them and appreciate them as part of the family.

If we love His Bride and lead her well, we will not intentionally do or say things that will cause pain, but we will at times react in word or deed that will result in offense.

Let's deal with these moments maturely and humbly so that all parties can move forward. My responsibility as a leader is to apologize for causing them pain. What the person does with my apology is their responsibility.

Romans 12:18 tells us as far as it depends on us, to live at peace with everyone. This implies that it will not always be possible, but as leaders we are to make every effort.

Dealing with my own discouragement

There will be days and seasons where we will battle against discouragement and will have to encourage ourselves in the Lord, because what surrounds us isn't doing the job. I deeply treasure the words and promises God has given me over the years and find these invaluable in times of discouragement. I have to make a decision to believe the truth of what He has said or the facts or feelings staring me in the face.

Sometimes the cost of leadership is showing up for the sake of those we lead even when we are wounded. This is not pretending everything is fine, but rather functioning from a place of strength in who God is for me and not how I'm feeling. Of course, it's okay to express times of weakness and ask for prayer from those we trust but remember that at times you have a parental role and not everyone you lead has the capacity to hear that you might be struggling.

I remember meeting with someone a while ago who asked me how I was doing. I decided to share that I was feeling rather discouraged over a certain matter. Their response was, "I'm so glad I'm not called to do what you do...let's talk about something else." This person did not have the capacity for me to be anything but fine for them. The conversation moved on to how they were doing.

When we find ourselves discouraged or wearing thin emotionally, it's wise to be careful who we spend time with and what we say yes to. As leaders, we are called to serve others, but they are not our master. Sometimes, it will be imperative to say no to certain requests if we have run out of margin. Take time to restore your soul and enjoy the company of your inner circle of friends. Ask them to pray for you and allow them to lift your arms as Aaron and Hur did for Moses when he grew weary. We were never meant to do this alone.

Exodus 17:12 NIV "When Moses hands grew tired, they took a stone and put it under him and he sat on it. Aaron and Hur held his hands up - one on one side, one on the other - so that his hands remained steady until sunset"

Reflection

1. Are there any wounds in your own heart that have come from people you lead? Give these to the Lord and trust Him for healing.

2. Are there any that you have offended? Ask the Lord to give you wisdom as to how to approach this. Sometimes we have to walk away and other times we need to initiate a conversation with the goal of rebuilding the bridge of relationship. His love never fails!

3. Identify those who restore your soul.

Remember . . .

You cannot afford to harbor offense.

Sometimes the cost of leadership is showing up for the sake of those

you lead, even when you are wounded.

Offense only hurts the one choosing to hold onto it.

14

Who does not call you leader?

Friendship is a Big Deal

Recently I was saddened to hear of a ministry colleague who had gone through a divorce and many of the team around them were not aware of what had been going on until afterwards. This is what can happen when leaders isolate themselves from authentic relationships where no one is close enough to ask how you're doing or notice when things are not quite right. It is a lonely and dangerous position and sets us up to fall into deception from the enemy about ourselves and our circumstances.

Years ago, while leading a large church we connected with other church leaders and realized one of the biggest needs in their lives was the need for friends. My husband and I started a group called Young Lions, and we invited those who were leading churches of over a thousand to meet together once a year to just connect and enjoy friendship. To this day, there are still strong friendships that were birthed from these times away.

We all need those with whom we can be vulnerable.

No matter what leadership role we are in, we all need those with whom we can be vulnerable. These relationships are a vital safe guard and a great and necessary support.

Here is a fascinating verse that speaks to the value of friendship for those in leadership positions.

> 1 Kings 4:1-5 AMPC "KING SOLOMON was king over all Israel. These were his chief officials: Azariah son of Zadok was the [high] priest; Elihoreph and Ahijah, sons of Shisha, were secretaries; Jehoshaphat son of Ahilud was recorder; Benaiah son of Jehoiada commanded the army; Zadok and Abiathar were priests; Azariah son of Nathan was over the officers; Zabud son of Nathan **was priest and the king's friend** and private advisor;"

Solomon held the highest position of leadership as King of Israel. In appointing his cabinet, one of the key positions is given to Zabud as the king's friend and private advisor. Solomon recognized the importance of friendship in his role so much so that he made it an official appointment.

Many are drawing from you, but make sure that there are some people in your sphere you can call friend.

Research proves that when we were knit together in our mother's womb, we were wired for healthy interaction with others.

Matthew D. Lieberman, director of UCLA's Social Cognitive Neuroscience lab, shared the following in his book, Social: Why Our Brains are Wired to Connect:

> "By activating the same neural circuitry that causes us to feel physical pain, our experience of social pain helps ensure the survival of our children by helping to keep them close to their parents. The neural link between social and physical pain also ensures that staying socially connected will be a lifelong need, like food and warmth. Given the fact that our brains treat social and physical pain similarly, should we as a society treat social pain differently than we do? We don't expect someone with a broken leg to "just get over it." And yet when it comes to the pain of social loss, this is a common response. The research that I and others have done using fMRI shows that how we experience social pain is at odds with our perception of ourselves. We intuitively believe social and physical pain are radically different kinds of experiences, yet the way our brains treat them suggests that they are more similar than we imagine."

Lieberman says that when asked about their most painful experiences, most people will talk about relational losses or hurts. On the contrary, most of our joyful seasons are often marked by positive relational interactions.

When God created mankind, He put in us a need to be loved and to belong. From the very beginning, He said it is not good for man to be alone (Genesis 2:18). Further on in scripture He tells us to love one another deeply (1 Peter 4:8). We are fearfully and wonderfully made with a God-given need to love and be loved. Most people who have suffered rejection or have been isolated from healthy affection are hurting people who hurt others. Psychologist, Abraham Maslow includes in his 5-tier model of human needs the need for love and belonging and intimate friendship. Roy Baumeister, a social psychologist, suggests that "Human beings naturally push to form relationships." His theory states that a lack of belonging can have a negative impact on our health, behavior, as well as our psychological health. It always delights me to see science lining up with the wisdom of our God.

We are wired for healthy and deep connection.

It is clear that we are wired for healthy and deep connection.

Emma Seppla, Ph.D, Science Director of Stanford University's Center for Compassion and Altruism Research and Education and the author of "The Happiness Track" states the following in her book:

Strong social connection:

- leads to a 50% increased chance of longevity

- strengthens your immune system (research by Steve Cole shows that genes impacted by loneliness also code for inflammation and immune malfunction)

- helps you recover from disease faster

- may even lengthen your life!

People who feel more connected to others have lower levels of anxiety and depression. Moreover, studies show they also have higher self-esteem, greater empathy for others, are more trusting and cooperative and, as a consequence, others are more open to trusting and cooperating with them. In other words, social connectedness generates a positive feedback loop of social, emotional, and physical well-being.

A little more on how science lines up with the word of God:

John 13:34 NIV "A new command I give you: Love one another. As I have loved you, so you must love one another."

1 Peter 1:22 NIV "Now that you have purified yourselves by obeying the truth so that you have sincere love for each other, love one another deeply, from the heart."

Romans 12:10 NIV "Be devoted to one another in love. Honor one another above yourselves."

We have looked at different levels of relationship in our lives and what they look like. We have seen that Jesus Himself had close relationships. He also ministered to many but didn't necessarily share His heart with them.

So, let's look a little more in depth at friendships in the context of ministry.

Many years ago, I was counseled not to make close friends within the church. They told me my only close friend should be my husband. While Greg is certainly my very best friend and confidante, he was never meant to fulfill all my friendship needs, nor me his.

I'm sure the comfortable sofas we see in malls are for the long-suffering husbands who graciously go shoe shopping with their wives for that perfect pair of new boots! At least they can find a comfortable place to wait as she wanders from store to store. We've all seen that worn out look waiting for her to find the treasure!

Going shopping with a girlfriend is usually a completely different experience. There's browsing and maybe coffee in between and much discussion on what is the best purchase.

I firmly believe that the Lord created us all to have good, healthy friendships with our same gender.

Over the years, I have been blessed with amazing friends. Some of my dearest friends are no longer on the same continent but with twenty plus years of relationship including years of raising our children, serving in ministry and doing life together, these women remain treasures in my life and those with whom I share my heart.

I have learned to give myself permission to have friends who I naturally connect with, regardless of "positions." I need these friendships to refresh my soul, and if you are in any form of leadership, so do you. Too many leaders burn out or get caught up in things that can destroy the very thing they are called to because they have no one close enough to reach out to for help or just cover them in prayer on a regular basis.

These women are the ones who encourage me, pray for me, make me laugh, share my victories, undergird me in difficult times and fulfill my God-given need for authentic friendship.

Most of my close friends have seen me beyond my role and pursued relationship with me, for which I am most thankful. Many will assume you are too busy and won't initiate connection. We can be responsible for this perception, so we need to be careful what we communicate. I encourage you to reach out to people you sense a natural chemistry with and pursue friendship with them.

Give yourself permission to build friendships within your own church or organization, even if you are leading it as long as these are not seen to be exclusive. We all need safe places where we can unstring the proverbial bow, talk about our struggles, our pain, and just be ourselves without our leadership hat on. There are times when I need a perspective from someone mature and trustworthy and other times I just need to have a good laugh or even a cry. Pursuing genuine friendship is vital to our emotional well-being.

We are to love each and every one the Lord brings to us, but we are not going to have a natural connection with all. This is normal and okay!

John 15:12 tells us to love each other as Jesus loves us. He died for all but He too had His closest friends with whom He shared His life.

Three hindrances to building authentic friendship

As we have looked at the profound value of having healthy relationships in our lives, there are also some mindsets and paradigms that can hinder us from experiencing good friendship.

1. Busy schedule:

Leaders by default spend much of their emotional energy caring for the needs of others and putting them first. By the time a number of fires have been put out, we have little time to just enjoy friendships that will refresh us. Not recognizing our need for this almost always results in loneliness and isolation.

A while ago, I met a friend for a scheduled lunch. I was excited to try a new restaurant and of course enjoyed our time together. On the way to take her home we talked about our need to get our nails painted for summer (very deep leadership conversation!) and decided to go and get pedicures right then. Driving home later, I realized that I could not remember when last I had done something spontaneous with a friend and how much I had enjoyed our afternoon of fun. It was an afternoon that refreshed my soul and reminded me of the importance of making time for friendship. No matter how busy we are, we must recognize that we are wired for connection and we need to make space to have authentic friendships in our lives.

> "Let him who cannot be alone beware of community. Let him who is not in community beware of being alone. Each by itself has profound pitfalls and perils. One who wants fellowship without solitude plunges into the void of words and feelings, and one who seeks solitude without fellowship perishes in the abyss of vanity, self-infatuation, and despair" (Dietrich Bonhoeffer, Life Together, 78).

2. Past hurts:

Leader or not, no one is exempt from relational hurt. If we are going to give our hearts in relationships, we open ourselves up to being hurt or offended somewhere along the way. Every relationship is a risk. I want to encourage you to always make a decision to risk again! Never fall into the, "I'm never going to open up to anyone again" trap of the enemy.

Offense only hurts the one choosing to hold on to it.

Offense only hurts the one choosing to hold on to it! So, let it go!

3. Looking for the one best friend.

Each of my friends adds richly to my life. I have friends who help me 'keep it real,' who I can laugh with until we are crying. I have friends who always have an encouraging word and remind me what

---

the Lord has said. (Guess who I call when I'm feeling discouraged?) I have a dear friend who thinks practically and strategically. Many times, she has helped me see the bigger picture and identify what is helpful and what is not. I could go on and on about all that has been added to my life through friendship. Only looking for the one best friend will hinder us from the rich treasures of a number of good friends.

Note: As leaders we always need to use wisdom as to what is appropriate to share with friends who are not on our leadership team. We do not have the luxury of complaining about leadership matters or people on our team to others.

On the teams that we have led, we have maintained a 'complain up' policy. You may not complain to someone about something happening on the team that is not in a higher leadership position. For example, in our context of local church, it would be not be right for an elder to complain to a member of the congregation about something they are not happy with. Of course, they are welcome and encouraged to come to us or another eldership member to talk about the issue and get it resolved.

Let me conclude this chapter with a quote from C.S Lewis in his book "The Four Loves"

> To love at all is to be vulnerable. Love anything and your heart will be wrung and possibly broken. If you want to make sure of keeping it intact you must give it to no one, not even an animal. Wrap it carefully round with hobbies and little luxuries; avoid all entanglements. Lock it up safe in the casket or coffin of your selfishness. But in that casket, safe, dark, motionless, airless, it will change. It will not be broken; it will become unbreakable, impenetrable,

Reflection

1. List two or three people with whom you have a natural chemistry for friendship.

2. Looking at the hindrances mentioned, are there any that might be standing in the way of you enjoying meaningful friendships?

Remember . . .

You will never go beyond needing people you can be vulnerable with.

You are wired for healthy and deep connection with others.

15

A Crown on my head

How Jesus related to women

Our church hosts bi-monthly events and an annual women's conference, and I continue to stand amazed at the caliber of ministry I see by women around me. Most of the messages are world class and delivered with anointing and revelation from heaven. I love seeing the younger women that I have mentored preach with power and confidence. I love releasing them to function in their strengths.

Jesus grew up in a strong patriarchal culture. From our vantage point, women were afforded little value at that time. At the temple they could not go past the outer court and were not permitted to read from the Torah. Men and women sat separately in the synagogue.

As we read the scriptures, it is clear that Jesus had little regard for the cultural norms of His day regarding women. We see Him blatantly defying the cultural norms and making a point of giving dignity and honor to women.

Jesus gave dignity and honor to the women He ministered to.

We need to catch God's heart for women and impart dignity and purpose to them just as Jesus modeled for us. At times, this might mean disagreeing with a religious norm or speaking boldly against rules and regulations that have caused limitations that our Father never intended.

Some women will come to us whole and ready to take on the world, but many will come broken and hurt because of abuse and harsh leadership even in the church. We have the awesome privilege of setting the captives free and leading the hurting to the truth of who Jesus is and how He sees them.

He longs to speak tenderly to His Bride and tell her that she's beautiful. How many desperately need to hear His tender and healing whisper!

> Hosea 2:14 NIV "Therefore I am now going to allure her; I will lead her into the wilderness and speak tenderly to her."

> Song of Songs 1:15 NIV "How beautiful you are, my darling! Oh, how beautiful!

Here are some of Jesus's personal encounters with women that so beautifully demonstrate how much He values us:

Woman freed from guilt

In John chapter 8, we find Jesus in the temple court teaching the people. This time, He's disrupted by the scribes and Pharisees as they bring a woman who has been caught in adultery to the middle of the court. They tell Jesus of her sinful act and that she should be stoned to death according to the Mosaic law. I can only imagine her humiliation as she is dragged before the crowds clutching a blanket or a piece of clothing to cover her nakedness. What does Jesus do? Instead of looking at her, he looks down, preserving her dignity, and writes on the ground with His finger. She is no doubt trembling with fear and embarrassment as the law keepers want to kill her and are testing the Teacher to see if he will uphold the law.

Jesus doesn't excuse her sin but rather He gives her a fresh start and removes condemnation from her. In John 8:10-11, Jesus gets up and asks her if anyone has condemned her. She says, "No one Lord!" His magnificent and freeing response is, "I do not condemn you, go and sin no more."

When people come to us, we can choose to restore their dignity and remove condemnation. We can be leaders who see potential beyond the problem and give people a fresh start just as Jesus did.

Woman at the well

In John 4, Jesus is on His way to Galilee from Judea. He's tired and stops to rest at Jacob's well in Samaria. A Samaritan woman arrives to draw water and Jesus asks her for a drink. He tells her of the living water that is available to her and also that she has had five husbands and the man she is with at present is not her husband. According to the Mosaic culture, a Jew was not allowed to speak to a Samaritan, let alone a Jewish man to a Samaritan woman! She recognizes Jesus as the Christ and goes into the town to tell others about Him. When they hear her story, they set out to come to Jesus. This woman didn't leave His

Presence condemned but rather excited to tell others about her encounter with Him.

When we reveal the true nature of God to others, they will run to spread the word of His goodness.

Mary, Jesus' friend

In John 20, we find Mary distraught outside Jesus's empty tomb, because the body of the one she loved was no longer there and she didn't know where he had been taken. When she recognizes Him, she calls Him Rabboni which means Teacher or Master. Jesus commissions her, who most Bible scholars believe was an ex-prostitute to bear witness of the risen Christ to His disciples. Jesus overlooked her past and saw her heart and deep love for Him. He could have chosen Peter, James, or John, but he chose Mary Magdalene and gave her a position of honor and dignity. According to Judaic law, a woman was not allowed to bear legal witness.

As leaders and ministers of His amazing grace, we too will meet people who love Him deeply and need to be set free from difficult pasts. We are called to be leaders who see what He sees and to treat people as though their sin has been fully taken care of by His blood.

Woman who received healing

In Luke 8:43, a woman who has been bleeding for twelve years and has spent all her money on doctors comes up behind Jesus and touches the hem of His garment. She is instantly healed and the bleeding ceases. It is important to note that in her culture, she was considered unclean and should not have been in public, but this woman is desperate and recognizes that He is the only one who could possibly heal her. She's trembling because she knows she shouldn't be out in public. What will the Jewish Rabbi say? Will he rebuke her?

What does Jesus, the Jewish Rabbi do? He calls her "daughter" and gives her identity and dignity and then tells her that her faith has made her well. He overrides the expected custom of the day and the religious interpretation of the law to show grace to her. His Presence brings peace and healing and transforms her life.

May we be leaders who tell those who come to us that He loves them, and sees them, and calls them His sons and daughters. May we tell others that He is the God who heals and that nothing is too difficult for Him!

Luke 8:48 NIV "Then he said to her, "Daughter, your faith has healed you. Go in peace.""

Mary Magdalene

In Luke 7:46, Jesus is dining at the home of a Pharisee. Mary Magdalene comes and washes His feet with her tears and expensive perfume. Jesus allows someone whom the Bible refers to as an "especially wicked woman" or "devoted sinner" to wash His feet. I can hear the Pharisees telling Jesus that this is wholly inappropriate!

Here is Jesus's response:

Luke 7:44-48 NIV "Then he turned toward the woman and said to Simon, "Do you see this woman? I came into your house. You did not give me any water for my feet, but she wet my feet with her tears and wiped them with her hair. You did not give me a kiss, but this woman, from the time I entered, has not stopped kissing my feet. You did not put oil on my head, but she has poured perfume on my feet. Therefore, I tell you, her many sins have been forgiven—as her great love has shown. But whoever has been forgiven little loves little." Then Jesus said to her, "Your sins are forgiven.""

Knowing that she wants to put her sins behind her, He tells her that her sins have been forgiven. We need to embrace our full forgiveness and then tell people the beautiful truth that all their sins have been forgiven and they are free indeed!

In all these stories, Jesus gives the women dignity and demonstrates His love for them. He was more interested in them being treated gently and receiving their healing and forgiveness than he was about upholding the customs of His day.

The enemy will always be at work to keep us focused on our weaknesses and reacting to his condemnation, because it dislodges us from responding to God's perfect love and experiencing the healing and freedom that is ours by inheritance.

His love never fails, it never gives up! Great is His faithfulness!

May we always lead from a foundation and revelation of His great love and compassion.

His love never fails; it never gives up! Great is His faithfulness!

Reflection

1. Explain how you have personally received a revelation of His love for you.

2. Which example of Jesus defying the cultural norms of His day resonated most with you?

Remember . . .

Jesus gave dignity and honor to women.

Like Jesus, leaders don't excuse sin, but always offer a fresh start by removing condemnation.

Choose to be someone who restores dignity to others.

PART 4
Dressed to Lead

In this section, we'll take a look at what is the best 'outfit' for us to wear to be effective leaders. When we are dressed appropriately for the occasion of leadership, everybody wins. When leaders are secure in who they are, those they lead will thrive. Even the tough conversations can end well when we lead clothed with love.

16

Kindness is a better fit

Dressing appropriately as a leader

A number of years ago, our family from England visited us in South Africa in December, which is the middle of summer. They came prepared with their new summer wardrobe for their trip. That particular year, there was an unexpected cold front along with snow and the wardrobe they had planned for their vacation was now of little benefit in the freezing weather!

When we stand in a place of influence over the lives of others, there are certain items of clothing that we are required to put on and some that we need to take off. Just as our choice of clothing can hinder or help us, what we wear as leaders will do the same.

What we wear as leaders will help or hinder us.

Can you imagine trying to hike in high heels or swim lengths while wearing a winter coat? Being dressed inappropriately can severely slow us down. The opposite is true when we wear the correct clothing for what we are engaged in. My favorite form of exercise is walking. As I walk most days, it is important to have shoes that fit well and provide the necessary support. When I'm properly clothed, I can walk for miles!

The scriptures are very clear about what we are to take off and what we should put on.

> Colossians 3:8 NIV But now you must also rid yourselves of all such things as these: anger, rage, malice, slander, and filthy language from your lips. 9 Do not lie to each other, since you have taken off your old self with its practices 10 and have put on the new self, which is being renewed in knowledge in the image of its Creator. 11 Here there is no Gentile or Jew, circumcised or uncircumcised, barbarian, Scythian, slave or free, but Christ is all, and is in all.12 Therefore, as God's chosen people, holy and dearly loved, clothe yourselves with compassion, kindness, humility, gentleness and patience. 13 Bear with each other and forgive one another if any of you has a grievance against someone. Forgive as the Lord forgave you. 14 And over all these virtues put on love, which binds them all together in perfect unity.

> 1 Peter 5:5 NIV In the same way, you who are younger, submit yourselves to your elders. All of you, clothe yourselves with humility toward one another, because, "God opposes the proud but shows favor to the humble."

According to these verses, these are the items of spiritual clothing that we take out of our wardrobe and off our shoulders because these items do not fit us as leaders and will be like the high heel shoes that will slow us down considerably as we walk out our call in Him. We are responsible to rid ourselves of these as they do not accurately represent who we are in Christ.

- Anger

- Rage

- Malice

- Slander

- Filthy language

- Lying

Now let's look at what we add to our wardrobe and what fits us well as believers and leaders who are new creations in Christ. These items of clothing are ours to wear as God's chosen people who are holy and dearly loved. They represent our true nature and will enable us to bear much fruit in our God given callings.

Compassion
Kindness
Humility
Gentleness
Patience
Forgiveness
Love

When our Heavenly Father looks at us, He sees us clothed in His righteousness.

Reflection

1. Are there any ill-fitting items of clothing that you're currently struggling with that need to be removed? Prayerfully ask the Lord to help you release these to Him so that you can walk in freedom.

2. Write down what you are choosing to put on that is tailor made to fit you as a child of the King.

Remember . . .

We are responsible to get rid of things that do not accurately represent who we are in Christ.

When our Heavenly Father looks at us, He sees us clothed in His righteousness.

17

Say yes to the dress

Agreeing with God's view of me

My daughter Nicole and her sister-in-law got married within a month of each other. Amidst all the wedding planning, there was a popular TV show called Say Yes to the Dress. In this show, brides-to-be try on multiple dresses with the hope of finding the perfect fit. As a mom, I remember the diligent search for the right dress. The style and fabric and fit had to be just right for the occasion.

In our own closets, most of us have items of clothing that fit us well and some that should probably go because they no longer fit or suit us.

As believers, there are things that we have already attained that are ours to wear because they fit us well, and things that are no longer fitting to wear as daughters of the King. For example, if we are wearing condemnation, we have to take it off because it no longer belongs to us. When the Lord looks at us, He doesn't see garments of shame but rather robes of righteousness. He is captivated by our beauty and doesn't see anything wrong with us. He longs for us to see what He sees both in ourselves and those He has entrusted us to lead. In His eyes, we are radiant and unashamed.

> Psalm 34:5 NIV "Those who look to him are radiant; their faces are never covered with shame."

One of our job perks is that we get to attend and officiate many weddings. I still get teary-eyed when I see the bride, radiant and beautiful and confident in the love of her soon-to be husband, come down the aisle, most often on the arm of a very proud father. I love seeing the groom's face as he beholds this vision of beauty. He is not thinking of her faults or weaknesses. At that moment, he is only captivated by her beauty. Your heavenly bridegroom is captivated by your beauty. As leaders, when we live in this revelation ourselves, we will walk in the authority given to us and will remove the grave clothes from our people, setting them free to wear what is rightfully theirs in Christ. When Jesus called Lazarus out of the grave, he came out alive but still dragging the grave clothes around his feet. In the same way, there are too many believers walking around with shame and condemnation and not enough leaders who are removing these and giving them the appropriate wardrobe of freedom and forgiveness. We can only give away what we have, which is why it is vital for those leading the Bride to be dressed appropriately.

We are called to remove illegitimate shame and to tell people that they are clothed with His righteousness.

Remove illegitimate shame by telling people that they are clothed with His righteousness.

If we are going to be life-giving leaders who set the captives free, we need to be most comfortable and feel most congruent in our own skin, in our new nature, because we can only impart what we have and believe ourselves.

Joseph

In the Biblical story of Joseph in Genesis 37, his father Jacob gives Joseph a robe similar to what was worn by children of royalty in that day. This robe was symbolic as we see later on in this story.

His older brothers strip him of it and Joseph gets thrown in a pit and sold to slavery.

A tactic of the enemy is to make us believe that we are not righteous because of our sin. Even though Joseph was a slave, he experienced God's favor. He was made chief warden and asked to interpret dreams.

The enemy can only deceive us if we believe we are slaves to sin and our circumstances. He has no power to remove our righteousness. As believers, we are clean and forgiven and we wear royal robes that cannot be stripped from us. The scripture is very clear that Jesus removed our sin and shame. He invites us to say yes to the dress He designed for us to wear. There is no other dress other than His righteousness that will fit us perfectly.

Later Joseph is released from prison and Pharaoh gives him his signet ring.

Genesis 41:41, 42 NIV Then Pharaoh took his signet ring from his finger and put it on Joseph's finger. He dressed him in robes of fine linen and put a gold chain around his neck.

Joseph is reinstated to his rightful place as a robe of royalty is placed back on his shoulders. As new covenant leaders we are called to reinstate His Bride to her rightful place and tell her that she no longer wears shame and condemnation and guilt but is clothed with fine linen and robes of righteousness.

> Ezekiel 16:9, 10 NIV "I bathed you with water and washed the blood from you and put ointments on you. I clothed you with an embroidered dress and put sandals of fine leather on you. I dressed you in fine linen and covered you with costly garments.

> Psalm 132:9 NIV "May your priests be clothed with your righteousness; may your faithful people sing for joy. "

> Isaiah 61:10 NIV "I delight greatly in the Lord; my soul rejoices in my God. For he has clothed me with garments of salvation and arrayed me in a robe of his righteousness, as a bridegroom adorns his head like a priest, and as a bride adorns herself with her jewels."

How does this impact us?

Let's look more closely at this incredible outfit that we as believers wear and place on the shoulders of those under our leadership.

If my husband officiates at a wedding that I'm unable to attend, the first question I ask is, "What did the dress look like?" If we are leading our people well, I believe this is what their dress should look like:

1. No condemnation to replace condemnation

Say yes to the dress : Agreeing with God's view of me

Romans 8:1 NIV "Therefore, there is now no condemnation for those who are in Christ Jesus,"

John 8:10, 11 AMPC "When Jesus raised Himself up, He said to her, Woman, where are your accusers? Has no man condemned you? She answered, No one, Lord! And Jesus said, I do not condemn you either. Go on your way and from now on sin no more."

Jesus gave her the gift of no condemnation and He has given us that same gift to give to those we lead.

2. Forgiveness to replace shame

My forgiveness is not dependent on what I do but on what Jesus has done for me.

Ephesians 1:7 NIV "In him we have redemption through his blood, the forgiveness of sins, in accordance with the riches of God's grace"

1 John 2:12 NIV "I am writing to you, dear children, because your sins have been forgiven on account of his name"

3. Total acceptance to replace judgement

Romans 15:7 NIV "Accept one another, then, just as Christ accepted you, in order to bring praise to God."

4. Joy to replace a spirit of heaviness

Isaiah 61:1-3 AMPC "THE SPIRIT of the Lord God is upon me, because the Lord has anointed and qualified me to preach the Gospel of good tidings To grant [consolation and joy] to those who mourn in Zion–to give them an ornament (a garland or diadem) of beauty instead of ashes, the oil of joy instead of mourning, the garment [expressive] of praise instead of a heavy, burdened, and failing spirit–that they may be called oaks of righteousness."

5. Healing to replace sickness

Isaiah 53:5 NIV "But he was pierced for our transgressions, he was crushed for our iniquities; the punishment that brought us peace was on him, and by his wounds we are healed."

A believer should never feel guilty or condemned for being sick. Having a sickness does not mean that you have sinned or that God is teaching you a lesson. It means that healing is for you and we trust God with you for your healing.

6. Authority to the replace defeat

Luke 9:1-2 NIV "When Jesus had called the Twelve together, he gave them power and authority to drive out all demons and to cure diseases, and he sent them out to proclaim the kingdom of God and to heal the sick. "

7. Power to replace powerlessness

Luke 24:49 NIV "I am going to send you what my Father has promised; but stay in the city until you have been clothed with power from on high."

We need to teach others that we live under an open heaven and all heaven's power, authority, and resources are available to us.

8. Peace to replace fear and anxiety

Fear and anxiety are always uncomfortable because they don't fit any more.

---

2 Timothy 1:7 AMPC "For God did not give us a spirit of timidity or cowardice or fear, but [He has given us a spirit] of power and of love and of sound judgment and personal discipline [abilities that result in a calm, well-balanced mind and self-control]."

People enjoyed being around Jesus because He is the Prince of Peace. Leaders who are confident in the Lord's love for them impart peace to those they lead. Peace fits us perfectly because we are His children and we are like Him.

2 Thessalonians 3:16 NIV "Now may the Lord of peace himself give you peace at all times and in every way. The Lord be with all of you."

9. Rest to replace striving

We are no longer striving to please God or work for His approval. When we wear this robe of righteousness, we rest in the love of our heavenly bridegroom. We don't have to work to earn His love.

Hebrews 4:9, 10 NIV "There remains then a Sabbath-rest for the people of God; for anyone who enters God's rest also rests from their works, just as God did from his."

Let's go back to our story of Joseph. His robe was made of fine fabric. It was different from his brothers' robes which were made of coarse fabric meant to be worn for hard labor. Joseph didn't have the same responsibilities as his brothers. He did not need to work in the field. All he had to do was attend to his father and enjoy their relationship. Joseph was found by his father's side, while his brothers were laboring under the hot sun. The only thing we are to labor for as believers is to enter His rest. This does not mean we don't work hard, but we work hard and see fruit because we are at rest. (Hebrews 4:10-11)

Galatians 3:27 NIV "for all of you who were baptized into Christ have clothed yourselves with Christ."

You and I are clothed with Christ bearing His characteristics of Power and Authority and Righteousness.

In summary

Just as Jesus gave the command to free Lazarus from the burial wrappings around his feet, I believe there is a command to leaders to free those we lead from burial wrappings of condemnation and shame. We have the privilege and authority to set our people free and launch them into His love and Grace.

John 11:43-44 NLT "Then Jesus shouted, "Lazarus, come out!" And the dead man came out, his hands and feet bound in graveclothes, his face wrapped in a headcloth. Jesus told them, "Unwrap him and let him go!""

In the last few years, I have walked closely with two beautiful, godly women who both came out of emotionally abusive marriages. Both have remarried amazing, godly husbands who treasure them. Their whole countenances have changed, and many have commented on how radiant they look, because they know they are loved. The Lord wants to romance us and tell us that we are loved and treasured. He removes all our grave clothes and then invites us to lead others in the same way.

Our weaknesses are covered by His blood. When He looks at you and me, He is captivated by our beauty because we stand radiant and unashamed in His sight, clothed in fine linen. As one called to lead, if you have not been sure of your place of victory, He wants to reinstate you to your rightful place so that you can lead confidently, knowing you are fully loved and robed in righteousness.

Reflection

1. Can you identify any areas where you carry shame and condemnation? Bring these to the Lord and let them go today, knowing there is no condemnation for you ever again!

2. Read through the description of what our clothing looks like. Are you settled in each of these characteristics?

3. Do you have a testimony of your freedom or someone you have ministered to?

Remember . . .

God is captivated by your beauty and doesn't see anything wrong with you.

You can only impart what you believe yourself.

Fear and anxiety will feel uncomfortable because they do not fit you anymore.

Peace fits us perfectly.

18

Living from the inside out

When secure leaders lead

For many years, I was convinced that I didn't quite measure up. I thought others should be leading because I didn't really qualify. I thought I had to have all the answers otherwise I wasn't a good leader. As I struggled with my own insecurity, I would prefer to arrive a little late to a social event with the idea that I would go unnoticed. It was extremely hard to be in a group of women, because I believed the lie that they really didn't want me there and that I didn't fit in. It sounds so ridiculous as I write this, but it was a painful reality for a number of years. Oh, what a joy when He delivered me from my fears and set my feet on the solid rock of who I am in Christ. Learning to live into who He says I am brought great freedom and fruitfulness.

As I began to believe I was who my Heavenly Father said I was and gained confidence to live into that, I stepped more securely into my true identity in Him. I began to believe that I truly am a daughter of the

King and that He has called and qualified me. I found great joy in releasing others to do what they loved and realized I didn't have to do it all. The scriptures tell us not to let anyone disqualify us, but so often we do this to ourselves and everyone we lead suffers.

Let's look more closely at this very real and debilitating issue of insecurity and how we can overcome it so that we can minister in the confidence that is rightfully ours.

Signs of an insecure leader:

- I internally compare myself to others.

- I find it difficult to celebrate others' victories because I believe they reflect my shortcomings.

- I find opportunities to point out the mistakes of others.

- I always pass the blame. It's never my fault.

- I often feel left out even if it's not true.

- I tend to seek sympathy from those I'm supposed to be leading.

- I do not easily build strong teams around me because I find this threatens my leadership.

- I do not easily release others to function in their gifting.

Insecurity in a leader not only hurts the leader but is destructive and limiting to those we are called to lead.

Leaders who are kind of insecure or egocentric, they basically sabotage themselves. John C. Maxwell

---

Insecurity in a leader is destructive and limiting to those we are called to lead, and to ourselves.

The root of insecurity is a lack of understanding of our true identity in Christ.

If we are going to be secure leaders, we have to change our core belief as to who we are and begin to see ourselves as our Creator sees us and believe we are who He says we are.

Romans 12:2 tells us that we are transformed by the renewing of the mind. Transformation and freedom come with a mind that agrees with what the Lord says about us.

Leading from a place of fear and timidity will hinder us from enjoying what God has called us to, and that which is meant to satisfy will only be hard and draining.

What happens when insecure leaders lead?

Insecure leaders seldom like to be challenged or questioned and find it difficult to recognize and celebrate another's strength. Sadly, the whole team is then limited to only the leader's strength and gifting. Craig Groeschel, founder and Senior Pastor of Life Church, says that when this happens the problem is no longer the problem, the leader is now the problem. Insecure leaders become the problem and the bottleneck.

Insecurity in leaders will hinder them from easily encouraging others and those they lead will seldom feel celebrated and empowered. Insecurity will often manifest as control, and the team become 'yes men' that fear their leader and will only move when he or she says so.

An environment of passivity and discouragement will be fostered by insecure leaders because input and perspectives from team members are seldom welcomed or considered. Insecure leaders will misread motives and ascribe that which is not true to those on their team.

Signs of a secure leader:

- I celebrate the strengths of others.

- I value team.

- I deliberately build strong teams around myself.

- I'm not threatened when others succeed but rather celebrate their victories.

- I love releasing others into what God has called them to.

- I'm not afraid of the tough conversations for the sake of the person and the church or organization.

- I can take blame and apologize when necessary.

What happens when secure leaders lead?

Secure leaders celebrate those they lead and love to see their team members bring their unique strengths. They welcome new ideas and different perspectives. A secure leader will recognize and deal with a problem at hand for the sake of the church or movement they are leading, regardless of how difficult it may be. They put what is best for others ahead of their own comfort.

Secure leaders encourage with ease and delight in empowering and releasing others. They surround themselves with other strong leaders.

Secure leaders will foster an environment of creativity and safety where ideas can be freely shared and considered because they know they don't have all the answers.

Secure leaders recognize and value the strengths that their teams bring.

Secure leaders recognize and value the strength that their teams bring. Even Jesus had a team.

Let's have a look at how Jesus led as a perfect example of a secure leader.

Jesus knew the value of a team because He was completely secure in the love of His Father. He purposefully discipled and raised up others. We see Him first calling Peter, James, and John, and then identifying the rest of His twelve disciples as His core team.

Jesus taught them to pray and minister in the authority that was theirs. He taught them to heal the sick and cast out demons. He let them be a part of multiplying food so many could eat. He sent them out with the key responsibility of pioneering His church.

Matthew 28:18-20 NIV "Then Jesus came to them and said, "All authority in heaven and on earth has been given to me. Therefore go and make disciples of all nations, baptizing them in the name of the Father and of the Son and of the Holy Spirit, and teaching them to obey everything I have commanded you. And surely I am with you always, to the very end of the age.""

Jesus was secure and humble enough to wash their feet. He had no need to lord it over them. Most importantly, Jesus was secure in His identity as the Son of God. He boldly stated who He is:

"I am the bread of life "

"I am the Way"

"I am the Truth"

"I am the Life"

"I am the light of the world"

Secure leaders do not allow others to define them negatively. They are secure in who God says they are and what He's called them to.

Secure leaders do not need the approval of men. Naturally we all enjoy encouragement and should give each other that, but our identity and security is in what He has called us to and who He says we are.

> 1 Peter 2:9-10 AMPC "But you are a chosen race, a royal priesthood, a dedicated nation, [God's] own purchased, special people, that you may set forth the wonderful deeds and display the virtues and perfections of Him Who called you out of darkness into His marvelous light."

> Exodus. 19:5, 6. AMPC "Once you were not a people [at all], but now you are God's people; once you were unpitied, but now you are pitied and have received mercy."

When we truly believe that we are chosen as His special people, that He calls us His own and has created us to display His beauty, we will lead from a secure foundation and those we lead will thrive.

> 1 Corinthians 3:10-11 NIV "By the grace God has given me, I laid a foundation as a wise builder, and someone else is

building on it. But each one should build with care. For no one can lay any foundation other than the one already laid, which is Jesus Christ."

If we are going to lead well, we must believe that we are competent and qualified to stand in our God-given space. The word of God tells us that our competence comes from God and that He has qualified us.

2 Corinthians 3:5 NIV "Not that we are competent in ourselves to claim anything for ourselves, but our competence comes from God."

Colossians 1:12 NIV "and giving joyful thanks to the Father, who has qualified you to share in the inheritance of his holy people in the kingdom of light."

Let's have a look at Ruth, a well-known Bible character. The word tells us that Ruth was a woman of strength and capability.

Ruth 3:11 AMPC "And now, my daughter, fear not. I will do for you all you require, for all my people in the city know that you are a woman of strength (worth, bravery, capability)."

You are strong and capable because of the Spirit of God who dwells in you

As a woman in leadership, you are strong and capable not because of what you do but because of the Spirit of the God who dwells in you.

You are fully capable and fully competent. Sometimes we can feel overwhelmed or believe that we are not able. This is why we need firm foundations based on the word of God. From this place we will be leaders who bring forth life and release many into their God-given destinies just as Jesus demonstrated when He sent His disciples out to change the world. As a secure leader, He released His authority to us to do all and more of what He did.

> Leaders become great not because of their power but because of their ability to empower others. John Maxwell

Reflection

1. Do you identify with any characteristics from the list of insecure leaders and secure leaders?

2. Take a few minutes and ask the Lord to show you how He sees you and rest in the truth that you are qualified to lead what He has called you to lead!

Remember . . .

Insecurity limits leaders.

Secure leaders celebrate others.

Secure leaders recognize and value the strengths of their team.

Don't let anyone disqualify you, not even yourself.

19

Yes you can

Women leaders in the Bible

Greg and I have been called to full time ministry within the local church. We lead together and recognize one another's strengths and giftings. He has never made me feel diminished as a leader because I'm a woman. Instead, I have felt free to lead alongside and in Biblical submission to my husband. This idea of submission is a subject on its own for another book, but if this statement is causing a negative reaction in you, let me just say that submission God's way is always intended to enlarge us and never to limit us. He always brings freedom, never bondage.

I have seen women flourish and enjoy their strengths in healthy environments, and I've ministered to many who have not been recognized, having been excluded, diminished, and deeply hurt because of their gender. I know of environments where the women are not invited to the leadership meetings. What a limited perspective this allows! These circumstances always stir up frustration in me because the giftings that are meant to add and enrich what God is doing are being dismissed.

> "More damage is done through poor church governance than anything else and more blessings come through good Biblical governance than anything else" (Beyond Leadership by Greg Haswell)

Leadership is meant to make a way for all and when it puts limits on people because of their gender, everyone loses.

When limits are put on people because of their gender, everyone loses.

Good Biblical church governance will bring great release to men and women alike.

> Psalm 68:11 NIV "The Lord announces the word, and women who proclaim it are a mighty throng"

> Psalm 68:11 TPT " God Almighty declares the word of the gospel with power, and the warring women of Zion deliver its message"

Walk with me through some passages in the Old and New Testament as we take a look at a few key women leaders.

Key women in the Old Testament

1. Miriam

In the book of Exodus, Miriam the prophet is leading women in song and dance, praising God for Israel's victory over the Egyptians.

Exodus 15:21 AMPC "Sing to the Lord for He has triumphed gloriously; horse and rider he has thrown into the sea"

Miriam prophesied through song and played an important role as a leader in Israel. Micah the prophet names Miriam, along with Moses and Aaron, as leaders who were sent to lead Israel out of Egypt and redeem them from slavery.

Micah 6:4 NIV "I brought you up out of Egypt and redeemed you from the land of slavery. I sent Moses to lead you, also Aaron and Miriam."

2. Deborah

Deborah is the second woman in the Old Testament to be called a prophet.

Following Joshua's conquest of Canaan, the Lord raised up judges to provide leadership, Deborah being one of them. She was recognized as a prophet and a judge and led the army of Israel to fight against the enemy. She also bore the title of Mother to Israel.

This powerful woman had religious, political, and military authority. Under her leadership, Israel enjoyed fifty years of peace.

3. Huldah

Huldah was a recognized prophet at a critical time in the life of Judah. When the book of the law was discovered in the temple, Josiah sent the following men to consult Huldah.

2 Kings 22:14 NIV "Hilkiah the priest, Ahikam, Akbor, Shaphan and Asaiah went to speak to the prophet Huldah, who was the wife of Shallum son of Tikvah, the son of Harhas, keeper of the wardrobe. She lived in Jerusalem, in the New Quarter."

4. Esther

Esther is one of my favorite heroines of the Old Testament. She was the Jewish queen of the Persian king, Xerxes, who through great courage and boldness saved the Jewish people from destruction. After the death of her parents, she was raised by her cousin, Mordecai. Esther prepares to go before the king and wins his favor because of her beauty and he places a royal crown on her head. Mordecai tells Queen Esther of the king's plan to kill all the Jews and pleads with her to do something. After calling a fast, Esther approaches the king and boldly asks him to spare her people. She tells him that Haman has plotted to kill the Jews. Haman is hanged and Queen Esther and Mordecai are given his estate. A decree was written to protect the Jews.

What a magnificent outcome of courageous leadership by a young woman who put her life at risk for the sake of her people!

Esther 8:7 NIV "King Xerxes replied to Queen Esther and to Mordecai the Jew, "Because Haman attacked the Jews, I have given his estate to Esther, and they have impaled him on the pole he set up."

Key women in the New Testament

1. Anna the prophet

Anna was an elderly Jewish woman mentioned in the book of Luke who prophesied about Jesus at the temple in Jerusalem. She was the daughter of Penuel from the tribe of Asher.

> Luke 2:36-38 NIV "There was also a prophet, Anna, the daughter of Penuel, of the tribe of Asher. She was very old; she had lived with her husband seven years after her marriage, and then was a widow until she was eighty-four. She never left the temple but worshiped night and day, fasting and praying. Coming up to them at that very moment, she gave thanks to God and spoke about the child to all who were looking forward to the redemption of Jerusalem."

2. Priscilla

Priscilla and Aquila were close friends of the apostle Paul and accompanied him on mission trips across Asia Minor and ministered in the church in Ephesus. They were in business, their trade being tentmakers, and they led a church that met in their home. Priscilla and Aquila co-labored with Paul in founding the church in Corinth and they were known by Paul as co-workers in Christ. Priscilla and Aquila are always mentioned as a team, which makes it clear that Priscilla's leadership and apostolic strengths were as recognized and valued as her husbands.

> Romans 16:3-5 NIV "Greet Priscilla and Aquila, my co-workers in Christ Jesus. They risked their lives for me. Not only I but all the churches of the Gentiles are grateful to them. Greet also the church that meets at their house."

3. Phoebe the deacon

Phoebe was recognized by the apostle Paul as a deacon in the church of Cenchreae. Paul chose Phoebe to deliver his letter to the Romans. When deacons were first appointed in Acts 6, they were to be of good character and full of the Holy Spirit and wisdom who were assigned to look after the widows who were being neglected.

Phoebe was a woman chosen by Paul to stand in this important office in the church.

> Romans 16:1-2 NIV "I commend to you our sister Phoebe, a deacon of the church in Cenchreae. I ask you to receive her in the Lord in a way worthy of his people and to give her any help she may need from you, for she has been the benefactor of many people, including me."

4. Junia, the apostle

Junia is the only woman in the Bible to be given the title of apostle. Not only was she an apostle, but Paul called her "outstanding among the apostles." The apostles traveled, taught, planted churches, and spread the word of God. Paul calls her a kinsman and fellow prisoner as she too suffered persecution and went to prison for the sake of the Gospel.

> Romans 16:7 NIV "Greet Andronicus and Junia, my fellow Jews who have been in prison with me. They are outstanding among the apostles, and they were in Christ before I was."

This is by no means an exhaustive list of women in leadership, but I believe these verses prove the point that God has called and intends both men and women to lead.

In Luke 13, Jesus is teaching in the synagogue and there is a woman there who had been bent over and crippled for eighteen years. When

He sees her, he calls her forward and says, "Woman you're free!" He lays His hands on her and she stands tall and upright again. I believe He calls us to freedom and longs for His daughters to stand upright and whole in their positions of leadership.

Your strengths, passions, and perspective are valuable.

You have strengths and passions and perspectives that are valuable and needed. You are free in Christ to be all He has made you to be!

Joel 2:29 NIV "Even on my servants, both men and WOMEN, I will pour out my Spirit in those days."

Reflection

1. Do you identify with a particular woman in the Bible?

2. What are your particular giftings or strengths? Make every effort to find yourself in a place where they are valued and celebrated.

Remember . . .

Christ-like leadership brings release to men and women alike.

You are called to freedom.

20

Better Together

The value of teamwork

When I look back over the years, I am so thankful for the teams we have served on and for those who have led us. We have spent hours and sometimes days with people of Kingdom capacity, wrestling and praying and implementing decisions. We have cried together over losses and rejoiced in the goodness of the Lord. We have worked hard together and celebrated success that could only have happened because we depended on strong teams. It is true beyond a doubt that we are better together.

Build teams

People in leadership cannot fulfill their mandate alone. We are designed to be team players. The kingdom's fruit of love, joy, peace, patience, kindness, goodness and gentleness function best in team environments.

We are most fruitful in team.

Simply stated, we are born again into a family and we are most fruitful in team.

Jesus modeled team work very clearly as he taught and trained and released His disciples. The godhead function together, each playing a vital role. Many leaders either burn out or get themselves into trouble that can deeply hurt many because they didn't recognize the power of team.

In the book of Ephesians, it tells us that we leaders are to equip our people for works of service. We are not called to create passive followers who only watch us perform but are never equipped and discipled to function in their own strengths. Each one in your team or sphere has something of great value to bring that will enhance and strengthen the assignment you're called to fulfill. I'm so grateful for the creative people, the strategic thinkers, the musicians, the teachers, and so many more that the Lord has added to our team over the years. We could not do what we are called to without these incredible gifts of strength. Make it a priority to build into your team, equipping them for works of service so that you can do the one thing that you're called and gifted to do. If finances allow, send them to conferences, buy books for them, and invest your own time into them to help them sharpen their gifting.

Make a point to notice and thank your team members for what they bring. A thank-you from you goes a long way. Many times, our team members are giving of their own finances and opening their homes and giving of what little time they have due to their own busy schedules. Though they are responsible to respond to what the Lord is calling them to do and to bring their strength, we are responsible to encourage, strengthen, and build our teams up.

> Ephesians 4:11-12 NIV "So Christ himself gave the apostles, the prophets, the evangelists, the pastors and teachers, to equip his people for works of service, so that the body of Christ may be built up"

Reflection

1. Identify the strengths of your team members.

2. How have leaders in your own life encouraged and equipped you?

Remember . . .

You are most fruitful in team.

Notice and thank your team members for what they specifically bring to the group.

21

That just went pear shaped!

Leading through the tough conversations

I wish there didn't need to be a chapter with this title, but because we lead people with deep feelings and sometimes differing opinions, this is an area that requires skill and intention. Too many people get unnecessarily hurt because tough conversations go pear shaped due to lack of leadership skill.

Over the years, I've learned some of these lessons the hard way. Here are some guidelines I've used to help me through the tough conversations:

1. Prayer

Always preface these times with prayer, inviting the peace and order of the Lord. We have authority to set atmospheres that allow for truth to be more easily received. Take responsibility to set an atmosphere in the beginning that is calm and in order.

2. Peace

Make a decision ahead of time to remain peaceful and even-tempered even if you don't feel like it! If all parties get riled up, no one will be heard, and all will want to argue their point. Remember, our perception is our reality.

3. Posture

Take a posture both in leadership and humility. When needing to address a difficult situation, where at all possible, give the person the dignity of their perspective.

A helpful phrase to use is "help me understand." For example: "Help me understand why you feel that way?" Or, "What motivated you to make this decision that has cost us?"

No matter who we are or what our perspective on a matter may be, we all need an opportunity to express how we feel. Make space for this. Give people their moment in court. When people feel valued and heard, they will be more open to counsel.

4. Praise

Amidst the conflict, find something you can genuinely praise.

For example, "I really appreciate how you remember the details of people's lives."

It's easier to move on to more sensitive ground from a place of authentic appreciation. No matter the issue, we want people to know we love and value them as our Heavenly Father does. The negative situation at hand does not define them or diminish their value.

5. Plan

Address the issue clearly and communicate what needs to happen moving forward.

Make your expectations clear so that they leave with a clear plan and purpose to prevent any misunderstanding in the future.

For example, "Next time you're unable to attend a meeting, please let me know ahead of time."

Strong leaders will come with strong opinions that won't always line up with ours.

If we are going to build strong leaders, they will have strong opinions that won't always line up with ours. They will bring amazing perspectives that we didn't see, and they will at times do things that we don't agree with or even sanction. I still prefer a strong opinionated leader over those who can't move anything or make any decision. Along with all the strengths will also come times of disagreement. It is vital to have a plan of communication so that conflict can be resolved in a healthy way.

Reflection

1. Which of these guidelines do you think you do well?

2. What would you like to do differently or better?

Remember . . .

In the midst of conflict, leaders are responsible to set an atmosphere of peace and order.

As you build leaders, do not be threatened by their strong opinions.

22

Right doesn't always feel good

Leading your team to do the uncomfortable

Waking up one morning many years ago in our home in Durban, South Africa, Greg turned to me and told me about a dream he'd had.

He explained how he saw the continents of the world shift. For a few months, the Lord had been speaking to me about going to the nations. This was all very well except that we were leading a growing church and up until this moment had not considered moving, especially to another continent! Three years later, with much confirmation from the Lord and many tearful conversations with friends and family, we boarded a plane to Atlanta, Georgia to pioneer Northlands Church.

Moving continents and leaving everything that is familiar is anything but comfortable, but uncomfortable obedience was necessary in order for us to walk into the next season the Lord had for us.

Uncomfortable obedience made a way for the church we left to gain revelation of His amazing Grace.

Uncomfortable obedience brought us into a deeper level of His Grace, and a dependency and humility in the Lord that one seldom learns in the spotlight. We have learned lessons in obscurity that we would not trade for anything.

Leaders have to lead. They do this by making the first move, voicing the uncomfortable call, and making the unreasonable ask of those who follow them. The Bible is full of leaders who made the uncomfortable choice. One of my favorites is found in the book of Luke where we find Jesus on the boat with Simon Peter and the disciples. They have had a long night fishing and have caught nothing. I'm pretty sure these men were exhausted and ready for a break. What does Jesus say to Simon Peter?

> Luke 5:4 NIV When he had finished speaking, he said to Simon, "Put out into deep water, and let down the nets for a catch." 5 Simon answered, "Master, we've worked hard all night and haven't caught anything. But because you say so, I will let down the nets." 6 When they had done so, they caught such a large number of fish that their nets began to break. 7 So they signaled their partners in the other boat to come and help them, and they came and filled both boats so full that they began to sink.

The command to lower the nets was given directly to Simon Peter as the leader. Their catch was dependent on his response, which was, "Because you say so, I will lower the nets." I can only imagine that these men were not thrilled with this idea and yet they did as Simon Peter commanded. They might have been thinking, "Really, Simon? Are you sure you heard right?"

Simon Peter made the call to obey, to do the uncomfortable. As we read further, we see that their obedience, their first move, led to such a large catch that they had to call other fishermen to bring boats to fill with fish.

Simon Peter's first move of obedience provided abundance for many. Most often there is overflow of blessings on the other side of uncomfortable obedience and the yes is dependent on the leader.

In this story we see some key leadership principles:

1. A leader's first and sometimes uncomfortable move, makes way for many to be blessed.

A leader's move makes way for many to be blessed.

---

2. People need to know the why of what we ask. Jesus told them why they needed to lower their nets: "Let down the nets for a catch." The clearer the why, the easier it is to lead our teams into blessing.

3. Simon Peter demonstrates Kingdom leadership when he says, "Because you say so." He is declaring that they are a team who respond to His voice above what they are feeling or experiencing.

I love the well-known story of Noah in Genesis 6. We have sung songs about the animals going in two-by-two and taught our children about how Noah built a boat as the Lord commanded, but have we ever stopped to think about the extreme discomfort of dealing with people's reactions to building a massive boat when there was no rain in sight? I wonder if Noah was ridiculed as a crazy old man as he obeyed God's command? Noah's uncomfortable yes led to the salvation of the world.

There will be times when we'll be positioned to make decisions and take actions that will not be comfortable for us or those we are leading. We will have to make a choice of obedience to say yes to our King even when it does not make sense. The joy on the other side is the overflow of blessing that we all get to enjoy and share. May we always be leaders who are willing to take the risks so that many walk in blessing.

Let's never forget the uncomfortable yes to the cross that made a way for all to be saved!

The uncomfortable yes to the cross made a way for all to be saved!

Reflection

1. Write down a time in your life when you experienced uncomfortable obedience.

2. What has been most helpful to you when guiding others to do what does not always make sense?

Remember . . .

Leaders make the first move in demonstrating obedience to the Lord.

A team who responds to God's call makes way for others to be blessed.

23

Who is next?

Raising the next generation

Recently, my mother moved into assisted living, and I flew to South Africa to help pack up her home. Sorting through many family photos, one in particular stood out. The Lord had brought this scenario to mind as I was preparing this chapter. As a little girl, I remember the baking of the annual Christmas cake and how we were taught to carefully measure each ingredient before adding it to the mix. We each wanted our turn to do what we had seen our mom do. I treasure this photo of my sister and me with my mom and grandma baking our cake.

I have yet to bake my own Christmas cake, but I'm thankful to have been raised in a home where there were many scenarios of the older women teaching the younger women, just as Titus 2:3-5 says.

Jesus modeled mentorship so well for us. He demonstrated ministry to His disciples as He cast out demons, healed the sick, raised the dead, and multiplied food. He then expected them to do the same and more. He told them that they would do what He did, and even greater things.

John 14:12 NIV "Very truly I tell you, whoever believes in me will do the works I have been doing, and they will do even greater things than these, because I am going to the Father."

Because we're leaders, people watch our lives and we have to ask ourselves, "What are we demonstrating? What are we expecting them to follow?" We stand in privileged positions of influence to build up and empower and release those we lead to do what we do and more.

As we mentor and model leadership for those God has given us, we want to give space to try new things. We want to communicate that we believe in their ideas even if they sound crazy! When we have a mindset to release others, we will witness things that we never thought possible. We will also be there to encourage them along the way when the great ideas do not work out as planned.

Winston Churchill said, "Success is not final, failure is not fatal: it is the courage to continue that counts"

Celebrate the victories as well as the boldness to try.

I love this quote from the Harvard Business Review:

"Mentors need to be givers of energy not takers of it. Consider why an idea brought to you might work, before you consider why it might not."

The value of mentorship and the raising up of the next generation is found all over the scriptures. Here are just a few of my favorite verses:

> Psalm 78:4-6 NIV "We will not hide them from their descendants; we will tell the next generation the praiseworthy deeds of the LORD, his power, and the wonders he has done. He decreed statutes for Jacob and established the law in Israel, which he commanded our ancestors to teach their children, so the next generation would know them, even the children yet to be born, and they in turn would tell their children."

Take time to recall the stories of His goodness, the victories after the battles, and the promises fulfilled. Tell of the times you held onto the word of God despite what you saw. Tell of the times you had to trust God for finances or healing and how you spoke truth into dire circumstances because you know who He is. These testimonies are tools in our hands to equip and strengthen the faith of those we are raising up to go beyond us. Psalm 78 tells us not to hide the things we have heard but to tell the next generation of the praise-worthy deeds of the Lord.

> Psalm 45:16-17 NIV "Your sons will take the place of your fathers; you will make them princes throughout the land. I will perpetuate your memory through all generations; therefore, the nations will praise you for ever and ever."

It is my hope and expectation that the people I walk alongside will go way beyond me.

It is God's intent that our sons and daughters stand on our shoulders, and it is my hope and expectation that the people I walk alongside will go way beyond me.

> Joshua 1:1-2 NIV "After the death of Moses the servant of the LORD, the LORD said to Joshua son of Nun, Moses' aide: 'Moses my servant is dead. Now then, you and all these people, get ready to cross the Jordan River into the land I am about to give to them—to the Israelites.'"

Joshua walked closely next to Moses as his aide. He had honored him and learned from him and then he was positioned to take the people into their promised land. The people we mentor are meant to go ahead of us and lead their generation into their destiny. They are able and equipped to do this when we believe in them and give them a godly example to follow. Let's be those leaders!

> Deuteronomy 6:5-7 NIV "Love the LORD your God with all your heart and with all your soul and with all your strength. These commandments that I give you today are to be on your hearts. Impress them on your children. Talk about them when you sit at home and when you walk along the road, when you lie down and when you get up."

A few years ago, we were invited to speak at a church and as we stood at the back, we could not help but notice it was mostly gray-haired people in the congregation. No one had deliberately invested time in raising up new young leaders to take the church into the next season. There was no succession plan and the organization was no longer growing.

When we're deliberate and excited about raising up the next generation, we will see great multiplication of what we have been given. If we are hesitant to train or pass the baton because we are threatened by the next generation, our ministries and organizations will have a very short lifespan as we cap and limit them to our gifting and lifetime. Ours is to release and never to limit. I will be so bold as to say that whenever we create a ceiling or do not deliberately make a way for others, we step out of the Biblical pattern of leadership. Because the Kingdom of God is an ever-increasing Kingdom, His intent is for us is to be leaders who work towards increase and multiplication as we pour into those coming up behind us.

The Apostle Paul models mentorship and raising up of a spiritual son so well in his relationship with Timothy. It would seem that Paul could go in peace knowing that what he had built would continue under Timothy's leadership as he had raised him purposefully to be his successor. Timothy, mentored by Paul, matured in his faith.

Acts 16:1 NIV "Paul came to Derbe and then to Lystra, where a disciple named Timothy lived, whose mother was Jewish and a believer but whose father was a Greek. 2 The believers at Lystra and Iconium spoke well of him. 3 Paul wanted to take him along on the journey, so he circumcised him because of the Jews who lived in that area, for they all knew that his father was a Greek. 4 As THEY traveled from town to town, THEY delivered the decisions reached by the apostles and elders in Jerusalem for the people to obey. 5 So the churches were strengthened in the faith and grew daily in numbers."

What does mentoring look like?

A mentor is one who helps another grow and develop in their area of strength. It is usually a long-term relationship that adds wisdom, teaching and practical opportunity. Timothy traveled with

Paul. A mentor will challenge perspective and broaden how we think and should always be one who encourages and cheers us on.

How we mentor will depend on the season of life, the dynamics of our ministries or organizations, and of course what works best for our individual personalities.

At times, I have led a formal mentoring group that has run for a period of time and covered a set curriculum. This is an effective and systematic way to impart knowledge and life skills around a specific topic.

In more recent years, I have mentored a number of young women who have asked me to do so. I meet with them individually and encourage them in their season of life and remind them of who God says they are.

I put a level of responsibility on them to press into our relationship, because if I'm more invested than they are it is probably not the right season to be pursuing a mentoring relationship. As Dr. Jack Taylor says, "You can be in the inner circle as much as you decide to be."

In closing, here is a summary of some helpful and key components to mentoring from the Harvard Business Review:

1. Put the relationship before the mentorship. There needs to be a base line chemistry and authentic relationship. Mentoring requires rapport.

2. Focus on character rather than competency. Mentoring must go beyond just the acquisition of skill to developing character and values.

3. Shout loudly with your optimism and keep quiet with your cynicism.

Remember, mentoring might require correction as we lead people out of behaviors and patterns that will be a hindrance to their calling and growth. These tough moments must be rooted in love.

Hebrews 12:11 NIV "No discipline seems pleasant at the time, but painful. Later on, however, it produces a harvest of righteousness and peace for those who have been trained by it."

As we mentor and raise up the next generation, we need to be well-grounded in God's love for us. Our rest in Him will be so attractive to those we lead, and it's from this place of rest and stability that we can partner with the Lord as we help others grow and put things in order in their own lives. May we be able to say with the apostle Paul, "Follow me as I follow Christ."

Reflection

1. List the names of people who have been most helpful in mentoring you and why.

2. Ask the Lord about who you should be raising up to walk in their destiny.

Remember . . .

Celebrate the victories as well as your boldness to try.

Your goal should be that those you lead go beyond you.

24

Courage under fire

Leading amidst our own pain

For as long as I can remember, I have always wanted to be a mom and dreamed of having children of my own. Pregnancy came much sooner than we had planned shortly after we were married. As much as this was quite a shock, we were also overjoyed as we announced our news to very excited grandparents. Sadly, I miscarried, but once we had tasted the idea of being parents, we decided it was time to start a family. Unfortunately, this began the painful journey of infertility and deep loss. Three years later after a difficult triplet pregnancy, I gave birth to three beautiful babies born too early at twenty-six weeks.

Our little girl, Sheraya, was stillborn due to pressure during the birth, and our boys Ryan and Jason lived for two and eight weeks respectively. A year later we were blessed with the gift a healthy, full term baby girl. Nicole Claire has been a dream daughter from the day she was born, and now she has a daughter of her own, our granddaughter Evangeline.

The circumstances of our lives and the hard places that we find ourselves in will have varying effects depending our perspective. During this most painful season, I realized that even though I had many unanswered questions, there was nowhere else to run except into the arms of my loving Heavenly Father. Sitting at the hospital holding our little Jason minutes after he took his last breath, the Holy Spirit stamped this on my spirit, "I will always be faithful to you." I have never forgotten that moment in the middle of great loss.

There will come times when we will find ourselves having to lead while dealing with our own personal crises. It might be something small like a disagreement with your spouse on the way to a meeting, a toddler who doesn't want to wear shoes today, a financial crisis, or a loss of someone dear to you. When we step into our leadership spaces, those we lead are most often unaware of the pain we might be carrying. I remember coming back to a leader's meeting two weeks after our last baby boy died and someone approached me and said, "It's good to have you back. I'm so glad you're over it." My cup of coffee almost found its way onto this dear soul's white shirt!

Here are a few things I have learned over the years about leading amidst our own pain:

1. It's not what we go through, but how we go through it

No matter what title or position we hold, we are not exempt from pain. What is on the inside will come out under pressure. At the beginning of this book, I addressed the importance of self-leadership. How we lead ourselves and our own personal walk with the Lord is what will sustain us and enable us to stand firm amidst the storms. We will make large withdrawals from our spiritual bank accounts in times of pain. Make sure to make regular deposits of His goodness and faithfulness. Ascribe greatness to Him often so that when the storms come, we remain well-anchored. How we publicly walk through trials can testify to the truth that God remains a good Father and is an ever-present help in times of need.

> Psalm 46:1 NIV "God is our refuge and strength, an ever-present help in trouble."

2. We don't have to have it all together all the time

There is a dangerous misconception in some circles that as a leader you must have complete control of your emotions and present yourself absolutely fine all the time. "But my people need me to be strong!" Yes they do, but they also need you to be real. Having vulnerable moments is not a sign of weakness but rather of great strength. When God gave us places of influence, He never called us to be robots with no emotions and perfect lives. When we are always fine, our people will struggle to connect with us. Jesus wept and showed anger and great joy. I can picture Him sitting around the fire with His disciples sharing a joke. There was nothing weak about His leadership!

> Luke 15:5-6 NIV "And when he finds it, he joyfully puts it on his shoulders and goes home. Then he calls his friends and neighbors together and says, 'Rejoice with me; I have found my lost sheep.'"

> Luke 19:41 NIV "As he approached Jerusalem and saw the city, he wept over it"

3. Have an inner circle

Identify your inner circle of friends and lean into them. Be bold enough and humble enough to ask for prayer and support when needed. Our default setting is to serve and minister to others, but there will be times when we need to be prepared and willing to be ministered to. Authentic friendships are invaluable to us because we all need safe places where we can lay down our leadership mantles. Let's give ourselves permission to not only give encouragement but to receive it when needed. There is a beautiful example of this in the book of Exodus. The Amalekites are at war with Israel at Rephidim. Moses tells Joshua to choose men and go out and fight with Amalek. While Joshua does as Moses has commanded him, he goes up the hill with Aaron and Hur. When Moses grew weary, Aaron and Hur brought a rock for him to sit on and held his hands up on either side. Moses recognized his need to be supported by his people and let them bring him strength when he was weak.

> Exodus 17:10-12 NIV "So Joshua fought the Amalekites as Moses had ordered, and Moses, Aaron and Hur went to the top of the hill. As long as Moses held up his hands, the Israelites were winning, but whenever he lowered his hands, the Amalekites were winning. When Moses' hands grew tired, they took a stone and put it under him and he sat on it. Aaron and Hur held his hands up—one on one side, one on the other—so that his hands remained steady till sunset."

Identify who holds your hands up. I have certain people in my life that pray for me and will stand in the gap for me when necessary. I know if I need them, they will be there. They are mature in the Lord and can carry the weight of me not being one hundred percent. Leaders are not exempt from needing support.

4.   We run

In hard seasons, we run either from God or towards Him.

We either run from God or towards Him. Pressure will always reveal what's inside.

During our hard season, in the span of one week, my grandmother died, my parent's divorce was finalized in court, and our third triplet, Jason, died. Like David, we had wept until we could weep no more.

> 1 Samuel 30:4 AMPC "Then David and the men with him lifted up their voices and wept until they had no more strength to weep."

There were days when I unwisely made threats to the Lord. Threats like, "If my last a baby dies, I'm leaving the ministry." But at the height of the crisis, deep down, I knew God was good and that there was nowhere else to go. I know in whom I believe.

That's what remains.

5. We strengthen ourselves in Him

Let's look at a specific time in David's life. He has just come from a place of siding with the enemy and is then rejected by the enemy, which is God's faithfulness to him. At the height of his distress, having wept all his tears, David turns to the One who He knows to be faithful and "strengthens himself in the Lord His God."

David, so weary of running from Saul, gives up and decides if he hides amongst the Philistines, Saul will leave him alone.

David and his men are exhausted and are heading home to Ziglag on a 3-day, 50 mile journey from Aphek to Ziglag. They are downhearted because they have been rejected by the Philistines. They arrive home to destruction and loss.

> The Amalekites have raided the Negev and Ziklag. They have attacked Ziklag and burned it, and have taken captive the women and everyone else in it, both young and old. They killed none of them, but carried them off as they went on their way. (1 Samuel 30:1-3 NIV)

> 1 Samuel 30:4 NIV 'Then David and the men with him lifted up their voices and wept until they had no more strength to weep.'

There are no children running out to greet them. No wives ready with a kiss. Their land has been burned to the ground and their families have been taken captive.

David faces a dramatic crisis as a leader. The men begin to turn against him and threaten to stone him. You can almost hear them saying, "If David hadn't made us go north with our Philistine enemies, this wouldn't have happened "or, "David should have insisted that some stayed back to defend our families."

David, along with these men, is in great distress and bitterly grieved.

When it seems like all is lost, the perception can be that God doesn't care; He's not for me. Some of you know what it feels like to be in that place, asking, "Can anything else possibly go wrong?"

6. Paul the apostle understood this too

2 Corinthians 4:8-9 NIV "We are hard pressed on every side, but not crushed; perplexed, but not in despair; persecuted, but not abandoned; struck down, but not destroyed."

In this moment, David stands apart from his army of men. He has suffered the same losses and shock that they faced but sitting in the dust with a tear-stained face, David knows that he must connect with the Lord His God. He knows he desperately needs his faith and strength renewed. He knows he cannot follow the journey of hopelessness.

7. David knew He had to reconnect with His God

1 Samuel 30:6 AMP "David was greatly distressed, for the men spoke of stoning him because the souls of them all were bitterly grieved, each man for his sons and daughters. But David encouraged and strengthened himself in the Lord his God."

8. Deep inside He knows His God

Sometimes the pressure of tough circumstances forces us to turn to what we know to be true. When I lost my babies, I knew there was nowhere else to run except towards the One who is always faithful.

Under pressure, David knew that his first task was to strengthen himself in the Lord and receive refreshing from His God.

Let me show you something fascinating:

Ziglag definition: There are two roots in the word:

One describes the exertion of pressure on something. The other means to pour out or melt.

The verb means to press someone mentally to bring out what's inside. The noun means an agent of pressure.

Ziklag was an agent of pressure in David's life that brought forth what he really knew.

We see what David contained internally when extreme pressure was applied.

What happens to you and me in the Ziglag circumstances?

I must confess at times that what has come out of me has been less than pretty. I've also been with people who demonstrate an extreme peace and unwavering trust even under the most stressful circumstances.

The good news is that because we have the Holy Spirit in us, we have direct access to His peace and patience at any time. We can be like David, and amidst great distress, we can find strength in our God.

Psalms 138:3 TPT "You strengthened me deep within my soul and breathed fresh courage into me."

9. We seek the Lord's voice

When David finds His strength in God, he asks Him whether he should pursue the enemy and is told to go after them. Ultimately, he recovers all that was taken. When we find our strength in the Lord, we will be leaders who hear our Father's voice and walk in the victory that is ours and, in turn, lead others to victory.

Reflection

1. Can you define a Ziglag time in your own life?

2. What did you learn about the Lord's character through this?

Remember . . .

In every circumstance, God will always be faithful to you.

In hard seasons, we run either from God or towards Him.

25

Storing Trust Chips

Leading with Integrity

Proverbs 3:3-4 TPT "Hold on to loyal love and don't let go and be faithful to all that you've been taught. Let your life be shaped by integrity, with truth written upon your heart. That's how you will find favored understanding with both God and men - you will gain the reputation living life well."

I was very close to my grandmother, Irene Cameron. Of her many characteristics, her integrity stood out the most. She was always kind, always welcoming, always ready with an encouraging word, and always pointed me towards "our Lord," as she called Him. Irene was a woman of prayer in all seasons and was completely trustworthy. She lived to be ninety-four, reading the Bible to those in her nursing home until the day she went to be with Jesus.

Integrity is a virtue that is essential for leaders who are going to bear good and long-lasting fruit.

Integrity is a virtue that is essential for leaders who are going to bear good and long-lasting fruit. Integrity is more than just being an honest person but being one who is always safe to approach. It is unsettling when leaders are as sweet as ever one minute and barely talking to you the next. It breeds insecurity in the team they lead. That kind of leadership does not win people's trust.

Integrity as a leader means that no matter how we might be feeling or what we are dealing with personally, we are able to dig deep and demonstrate peace and kindness without leaking our frustration onto others. When leaders allow their erratic moods to dictate how they lead, their followers suffer.

Integrity is an adherence to ethical principles regardless of pressure or possible loss.

Integrity is an adherence to ethical principles regardless of pressure or possible loss.

Honesty is key. People need to be able to trust what comes out of our mouths. Too many people have been wounded by leaders who were found to be hiding the truth.

Integrity comes from the Latin word, "integer," which means whole and complete. Whole leaders are settled in who they are and don't need to pretend to be something they are not. When we're settled in our own identity in Christ, we will be the same person publicly and privately. Over the years, I have seen a number of leaders fail because they were trying so hard to portray to their followers someone they were not and couldn't keep up the facade.

One of our personal core values is authenticity. People are a lot more discerning than we sometimes give them credit for, and people will soon discern who we really are.

Leadership requires that we are intentional about walking in integrity. It means that we are quick to apologize and walk in humility when we are wrong.

Leaders of integrity make conscious and sometimes tough decisions to do the right thing regardless of opposing opinion or circumstances.

Integrity is an adherence to ethical principles regardless of pressure or possible loss.

What we model will multiply.

What we model will multiply. If we want a spirit of integrity in our sphere, we need to be leaders whose lives demonstrate this core characteristic. Those we lead will catch what we have because we have authority to influence.

Everything we do as leaders is magnified. Our people are watching us more than we realize. How we stand for truth, how we lead under pressure and remain calm and consistent, and how we humble ourselves to apologize are all magnified and will influence others to do the same.

Our greatest example of integrity is found in the pages of the Bible as we read about Jesus's life. He demonstrated integrity to the core when He looked at the cross and said the toughest "yes" in all of history. He knew the reality of the death that faced Him. He chose this "yes" for the sake of those He loved. He was truly a man of His word!

"The supreme quality for leadership is unquestionably integrity. Without it, no real success is possible, no matter whether it is on a section gang, a football field, in an army, or in an office" Dwight D. Eisenhower, 34th President of the United States

Reflection

1. Name three people in your life who come to mind when you think of people of integrity.

2. How can you best model integrity to those you currently lead in your home, business, church, or organization?

Remember . . .

Integrity is essential to long-lasting leadership.

What we model will multiply.

26

Clamming Up

Keeping Confidences

Proverbs 11:13 NIV "A gossip betrays a confidence, but a trustworthy person keeps a secret"

Proverbs 21:23 NIV "Those who guard their mouths and their tongue keep themselves from calamity"

I have been made rich by the many amazing women the Lord has added to my life. I'm so thankful for each friend, mentor, and spiritual daughter who add so much joy to my journey. I wouldn't want to do life without them!

Many of these women are like clams. If you have ever tried to pry open a clam shell, you will know it requires a clam knife to cut through the muscle with skill. I know, without having to ask for it, that my heart is safe with them because what I share will remain with them only. I also know that I will not be defined in my moment of weakness because they know who I am in Jesus.

It is my desire to be a safe place for people to share their lives with me—the good, the bad, and the ugly—just as my friends are for me. Keeping a confidence means that unless what someone shares is endangering their lives or those around them, the vulnerable moments they share with me are private.

When counseling, assume the conversation is confidential unless otherwise stated.

A cost of leadership is keeping things confidential. We are going to be privy to information that others might not know, and people need to know that we can be trusted with what they tell us.

Some of what is shared might be exciting news of a pending engagement, a baby on the way, or a new opportunity. There might also be times when people confide in us and share something morally or ethically wrong. If the information disclosed involves abuse of any kind, suicidal tendencies, or endangerment to themselves or anyone else, we are obligated to share this with those who can step in and help. (Most times this will require seeking professional help and sometimes a report). These create difficult moments, because we suddenly have a responsibility to break a confidence.

Here are some phrases that might be helpful in these circumstances.

"I value your privacy and your trust in me, but I'm unable to keep what you're telling me between us."

"I care too much about your safety/your reputation/this church/this business to do nothing about this."

"I would suggest you go and speak to_____. I'm happy to go with you."

For the most part, assume the conversation is confidential unless otherwise stated. If you think it would be helpful for others to be involved, you can say, "Would you mind if I mentioned this to someone," or "I suggest you speak to_____."

There will be times when you might need another perspective to give better counsel. Let the person know you will be doing this when at all possible.

Can I talk to my spouse about what I have been told?

As a general rule, I will not commit keeping something from my husband, because very often he will help me process something I have heard. Many times, the counsel I give includes his perspective. Of course, if women share intimate details with me that they'd rather I keep private, I will not share them, just as he won't with me when men confide in him. Use your discretion when it comes to sensitive issues, but let people know that if you're married, you're not in the habit of keeping things from your spouse.

God's heart on this matter

It fascinates me that the God of the Universe has secrets and He also has certain people that He confides in. The scriptures tell us that He confides in those who fear Him.

Psalm 25:14 NIV "The Lord confides in those who fear Him;
He makes His covenant know to them"

There are deep truths about who He is and what He has done for us that He longs to share with those who will listen. Jesus tells His disciples that the secrets of the Kingdom have been given to them. He entrusted them with revelation and understanding of eternal matters that He did not share with the crowd.

Matthew 13:11 NIV "The knowledge of the secrets of the Kingdom of heaven has been given to you, but not to them"

Our Heavenly Father loves to tell us things about what He's doing and share things with us as to how we can pray into certain circumstances. Many times, He will share details with us because He trusts us to pray for our brothers and sisters, and He knows that we will not share with others what He has revealed to us.

May we be like Moses, who not only knew His deeds but understood His heart. God trusted Moses with His ways. There are times when the Lord will whisper His ways to us because He trusts us to treasure them.

Psalm 103:7 AMPC "He made known His ways to Moses, His acts to the children of Israel."

Reflection

1. Identify a few clams in your own life. Share your appreciation of them for being so trustworthy.

2. Ask the Lord to share His heart with you for a certain matter or person.

Remember . . .

A cost of leadership is keeping confidences.

God wants us to see what He's doing and understand why.

27

A few last thoughts

Personal Testimony

A s a young woman, I believed the lie that I was not liked and that most people only tolerated me because this was the Christian thing to do. This had nothing to do with my home life, as I was always affirmed and well-loved by my parents. In middle school, I attended class overseas, and I was the strange girl with the funny accent.

These early years definitely played a role in letting a seed of rejection take root. As a young adult, well into my twenties, I did not enjoy large social events and tried to arrive late so as not to be noticed. Sitting alone at any given function was tortuous, as it just confirmed the lie of rejection.

When I came to realize how much my heavenly Father loves me and always approves of me, I was set free from believing the lie of rejection. I'm so thankful for this, because I know this insecurity would have hurt others in my path. This mindset had the potential to bring damage and hinder what God has called us to. Now, I have the privilege of telling others about their true identity in Christ.

Anxiety and some awful panic attacks were something I battled for a number of years as an adult and church leader. I know the pain and reality of this but also know the freedom and peace that is ours by right as His daughters. Too many leaders suffer in silence with whatever their struggle and never admit to any weakness, all the while holding on by a thread. I know the feeling of sitting through meetings and hoping no one will notice that it's taking everything inside of me to just stay in the room!

One day, we were standing in a circle as a leadership team praying for a conference we were leading for adoptive parents. As we prayed for the Lord's peace for these families, I suddenly felt like I was about to fall asleep on my feet. As I walked away, I asked the Lord what that was. I heard Him say, "That was my peace, which is also for you." Something changed that evening, and the power of anxiety over me was broken. There are times when I still feel the push of the enemy to pull me back into that place, but I know that anxiety and fear do not have a hold on me. I have come to realize and embrace the Truth that the peace of Heaven is mine and dwells in me. The Holy Spirit lives in us all as believers and therefore His peace, His patience, and His joy are always ours. We are, by definition, peaceful people because we carry Heaven's peace. This revelation has radically altered my life. When I feel a wave of fear, I lean into what is mine by right!

I share these testimonies with you to encourage you that if any of the above is your struggle too, there is beautiful and sustained deliverance for you. You are called to lead in peace and enjoy great fruitfulness in all you put your hands to. Happy leading!

Notes

Chapter 1

Heidi Baker, **There is always enough:** Published in the USA in 2003 by Chosen Books, A Division of Baker Books Company

Chapter 6 & 7

Wayne Cordeiro, **Leading on Empty**: Refilling your tank and renewing your passion
Bethany House Publishers 2009

Chapter 14

Matthew D Lieberman, **Social, why our brains are wired to connect.**, Crown Publishers 2013
Emma Seppala, **The happiness track**, HarperCollins Publisher 2016
Dietrich Bonhoeffer, **Life Together**, Harper & Row Publishers 1954
The Four Loves, C.S Lewis, Harper Colllins Publishers 1960

Chapter 19

Gregory Haswell, **Beyond Leadership**, The governmental role of the attendants of the bride, Deep Roots Press, 2013

Made in the USA
Columbia, SC
10 July 2021